Tom Sullivan's
Adventures
in Darkness

Derek L. T. Gill

Other Books by Tom Sullivan
If You Could See What I Hear
    with Derek L. T. Gill
You Are Special

ISBN 0-8249-8021-2 395

Copyright © MCMLXXXI by Tom Sullivan and Derek L. T. Gill
All rights reserved
Printed and bound in the United States of America

Published by Ideals Publishing Corporation
11315 Watertown Plank Road
Milwaukee, Wisconsin 53226
Published simultaneously in Canada

Contents

The Spook House 5

Seeing Without Eyes 11

Lost in the Fog 21

Tucky and Other Friends 31

Learning to Live 39

How to Play the Game 51

The Dream of Tomorrow 63

A Giant Step 74

Falling in Love 88

My First TV Appearance 99

Vision Unlimited 108

Reaching for Life 121

Epilogue 125

This book is dedicated to my school friends and my teachers who, with my family, helped me to find such exciting adventures in darkness.

The Spook House

I was awakened by the sound of the foghorn. That meant that Mr. McDonagh would not be taking me fishing, I thought, as I stretched in semiconsciousness. Whenever the fog swept in from the Atlantic Ocean, no boats left the harbor.

I lay back in bed with my hands behind my head, wondering what I could do instead of going fishing. There had to be something exciting to do. I couldn't waste a whole day of summer vacation doing nothing. Oh, well, I thought, the gang will come up with a good idea.

Mom was calling me for breakfast. I dressed hurriedly and went downstairs. I had just sat down when the doorbell rang. It was my friend Tommy Healey.

"Want to go bicycling?" he asked.

"Sure," I replied, with my mouth full of toast.

"You'll have to be careful," said Mom. "It will be dangerous in the fog."

Dangerous for whom, I thought, since I was blind and couldn't see anyway—but, of course, other people couldn't see us if it was foggy.

I finished my breakfast and Tommy wheeled my tandem bike off the porch. A few minutes later we joined the other members of our gang—John Francis, Frankie Bakey, and the Turnbull twins. We were all eleven years old, except for Frankie; he was twelve. If the sun had been shining, we would have gone swimming. We thought about playing basketball, then Frankie said, "Let's go to the Spook House."

He was referring to a rambling, clapboard house constructed like a ship, about two miles down a dirt lane near the beach. We had been there before—but never inside. Nobody ever went inside the Spook House! There were tales about an old sea captain who had lived there many years ago. Even though the windows had been boarded up, some people said that they had seen lights in the house at night and had heard groans coming from inside.

I sat on the back seat of the tandem with Tommy up front, and the others mounted their own bikes. The dirt road was bumpy and potholed; and in the distance, the foghorn wailed.

When we arrived, we leaned our bicycles against the broken-down fence. Then John asked quietly, "Do you think there really is a ghost?"

"My big brother says there is," replied Tommy Healey.

"Only one way to find out," said Frankie. "One of us has got to go inside."

Because he was a year older than the rest of us,

The Spook House

Frankie had always been the leader of our gang; but I suspected that he was too frightened to look for the ghost himself. This was my chance to show that I was braver than Frankie, so I spoke up quickly before I lost my nerve.

"I'll go," I said, but hoped the others couldn't hear my heart thumping.

"You're blind. You won't be able to *see* the ghost," said Frankie.

But when he dared each of the other members of the gang to enter the Spook House, they all refused.

"Okay, Tom," said Frankie, as he turned to me. "You go; you can tell us if you hear anything."

"Or feel anything," shivered John. "Spooks are supposed to have cold, clammy hands. I remember reading about their hands."

One of the gang picked up a pole from the broken-down fence and prodded me down a brick path that had weeds growing between the cracks. I could feel the weeds brush against my legs. The gang stopped when we reached the steps leading to the porch.

"Okay," said Frankie. "Three steps up, and the door is right in front of you."

I felt my way forward. The rotten planking of the second step gave way and I fell down. My courage wavered; there was still time to turn back. But I had accepted a challenge, so I kept on until I reached the front door. It was locked.

"There's a window to your right; knock out the board," urged one of the Turnbull twins. I moved down the porch and felt the plyboard covering a window. It took some pulling and prying before the plyboard finally gave way, but the effort covered up my anxiety.

I wasn't going to let the gang see I was trembling with fear as I vaulted through the window. Inside, the dank smell of age floated to my nostrils. Outside, the others were talking in whispers as they waited for some outcry from me. They were expecting a bloodcurdling scream.

I felt my way across the room by waving the stick in front of me. The floorboards creaked. Suddenly, there was a rustle in the corner and a scampering across the floor. I waited for clammy hands to seize my throat. It was only a rat, but it sounded like the sort of shuffling I imagined a ghost would make.

I clicked my tongue against the roof of my mouth. That is a technique I had learned to use to interpret my surroundings. The echo told me that the room was long and narrow. I pressed the stick against the wall and then scraped it along torn wallpaper until I found a door. This door opened at a push and I knew I was in a hallway. Tapping along with my stick, I discovered several doors leading off the hall. In the next room I bumped into something solid and put my hand out to keep from falling. A dissident chord rang out. My hand had pressed against the keyboard of a piano.

"Hope the ghost likes music," I said to myself. The gang told me later that when they had heard the piano, they believed it was chains rattling.

When I tried to leave this room, I couldn't find the

The Spook House

door. Twice I tapped the stick against the four walls, but for some reason, I kept missing the door opening. I felt a moment of panic. I thought I was trapped, so I shouted for help; but none of the gang came to my aid. I stopped and listened; the silence was total. Then, very faintly, I heard a robin singing. I guessed that the birdsong had to be coming through the broken window. By pausing every few steps to listen, I found my way back to the hall and then to the window through which I had entered the house.

I suppose that if I had really been lost inside the Spook House, someone would have rescued me. But I like to think that a little bird saved me from being strangled by a long-dead sea captain who did not like trespassers.

As I climbed back through the broken window onto the rickety porch, I felt like a real hero. Not even Tom Healey's big brother had ever dared to enter the Spook House. At that moment, however, another sound sent my blood pulsing once again. It was a police car siren. Someone must have seen us and reported to the police that a gang of boys was trespassing.

"What are you boys doing?" shouted the cop. I had been following regularly a crime serial on the radio, and I knew that when you were caught by the police you had to have a quick answer. I was first to speak.

"We've just been sunning ourselves," I said.

The policeman was not impressed. He bundled us all into his car and drove us to the station. I had forgotten that it was a foggy day.

At the station, we had to give our names and addresses and telephone numbers. The officer in charge at the desk phoned our parents. The other parents arrived quickly, but my dad told the officer to "cool me off in a cell." So, for the next two hours, I sat on a bench behind bars; and I decided then and there that I preferred the dank smell of the Spook House to being locked in a cage.

When Dad finally arrived and drove me home, he laughed and laughed. He seemed quite proud that his young son had been in jail. I didn't think it was so funny.

"The best way to learn life is the hard way," he said, hoping, I suppose, that I had learned an important lesson that day.

I was proud too, but for a different reason. I was proud because I was elected to be the leader of the gang instead of Frankie Bakey. I think some of them believed me when I told them how I had fought off the ghost with my bare hands. Of course, I couldn't tell them what the sea captain looked like; but I described in detail how I tugged at his beard and somehow managed to escape, wrenching his clammy fingers from my throat.

"Yeah, we heard you scream," said Frankie.

"That wasn't me screaming," I boasted. "That was the ghost."

Seeing Without Eyes

I am really quite lucky to be alive. I was born three months too early and weighed only three pounds—less than half the weight of most newborn babies. If I had been born two or three years earlier, I probably would not have survived. But in the hospital in West Roxbury, Massachusetts, where I was born, they had just installed a newly invented incubator. This looked like an empty aquarium—a sort of glass-sided box in which premature babies were placed. Inside the incubator, the temperature could be kept the same as blood temperature; and a supply of oxygen was pumped into the incubator so that the baby could breathe.

    Too much oxygen was pumped into mine, although at that time we believed that a high concentration of oxygen was necessary to support the incubator baby. Technology has since perfected human incubators, but my eyes were irreparably damaged. The result was rather like exposing film to light before it is placed in the camera. The film will no longer record an image coming through the lens.

At nine months, Tom was beginning to learn the feel of his yard as he reached out to touch the bush.

A day after I was placed in the incubator, my eyes stopped recording images. I was blinded, but I was not alone. Many thousands of premature babies born that same year were blinded also. Yet, if there had been no incubators, many of us would have died. I am blind, but I am alive!

So, that is why I say I am lucky.

You may ask, "What is it like to be blind?" Well, perhaps as you read about the adventures in my life, you will have some idea of what it is like. Oh, there are the frustrations and heartaches; but more importantly, there are the excitement and successes.

Most people have five senses with which to record data in their memory bank—sight, hearing, touch, taste, and smell. Sight is obviously the most crucial of them

Seeing Without Eyes

all. Eyes are windows on the world. With them, a child soon discovers color and form and movement. He recognizes the faces of his parents and his brothers and sisters. When he learns to walk, he sees which way to go and how to avoid things which may hurt him or trip him up.

If you talk to me about light and color—about blue and green and red—I don't really know what you mean. Those are just words to me, like blue sky, red apple, green grass. I know how an apple feels, and how it smells, and how it sounds and tastes when I bite into it; but I can't tell if one is green or yellow or red. I have had to discover the world with only four senses—touch, sound, taste, and smell. With a blind person, these senses usually become more highly developed, important, and useful.

Many animals learn how to "see" with their other senses. For instance, bats are blind; but they can fly about a room without crashing into a wall. Bats make a high-pitched squeak at regular intervals, which echoes from their surroundings. From the echoes they can determine the location and the distance of any obstacle. The same principle is used in radar to track aircraft and in sonar to explore the ocean floor.

Today, radio telescopes, which pick up echoes bouncing back from space, are able to map the surface—the mountains and valleys—of distant planets. Before the astronauts first landed on the moon, radio telescopes had already located the best landing sites.

I have been told that when a dog chases a rabbit, the

dog does not look up at his quarry but keeps his nose to the ground as he follows the scent.

My ears and my nose send a stream of messages to my brain all the time, and I'll bet I notice things that many people miss—or else ignore. Have you ever heard a snowflake fall? I have. How do I know when it is safe to cross the street at an intersection? I can hear the traffic lights changing, and I can tell from the sound of the vehicles in which direction the traffic is moving.

When I was still a child, I used to play hide-and-seek with an uncle; and I could always find him, even when he hid in a closet. He smoked cigars; I simply followed my nose.

When I was older, I played more exciting games and even gained a national title. But I will be telling you about these adventures in later chapters. I am remembering now the time when I witnessed a murder. When I say witnessed, I do not mean that I saw it happen, even though I knew it happened. I was in a parking lot and I heard two men fighting. One of the men fell and the other ran away. I will never forget the sound of those running footsteps. Perhaps one day I will hear them again and will help to bring the murderer to justice. It was a frightening experience.

When you have to use your ears for eyes, you discover that different people walk differently, just as they talk differently. You can often tell as much, and perhaps more, from the way a person speaks as from the way he looks. A person can smile but really feel very sad or angry or tired or bitter. A smile can lie, but the sound of a voice

Seeing Without Eyes

rarely does. People in general tend to forget that, or perhaps they never really noticed.

So, in many ways, a person like me often knows more about what is going on around him than does a person who uses only his eyes.

The sense of touch can be very exciting. For instance, a handshake is often quite revealing. Once I have shaken hands with someone, I can tell a great deal about him. A limp handshake usually means a person is unsure or tired or not very interested. But when a good friend shakes hands, he usually holds onto my hand a moment or two longer and he pumps my hand up and down.

After shaking hands with someone, I often have fun guessing the person's height and weight. When he speaks, I know at what level his mouth is, so I know how tall he is. If his fingers are pudgy and long, then he is likely to be heavier than a person whose fingers are thin and short. When I guess a person's weight within a pound or two, onlookers think it is incredible. It isn't, of course. Anybody can learn this trick.

There are many interesting games you can play with your friends to test their ability to "see" with their ears, their noses, and their fingers. For instance, on a tape recorder you can record familiar sounds, like the shwoosh of brushing teeth, the striking of a match, the whirr of a vacuum cleaner, and the flutter of thumbing your fingers through the pages of a book. Then find out how many of your friends can guess what these sounds are.

A similar game can be played to test how sensitive

one's fingers are. Blindfold your friends and have them feel a seashell, a fir cone, a piece of chocolate, a candle, an electric light switch, and so on.

These can become more than games. They can be exercises which help you develop your other senses to a higher degree. Once all your senses are working well, every day becomes much more interesting and exciting. I know I find that to be true.

Take reading, for instance. Almost everybody, at one time or another, has seen a blind person reading a book that is written in Braille. Braille is a system in which letters and words are made with tiny raised dots on paper. Using the fingertips, a blind person can read Braille as easily as you are reading these words with your eyes.

I love to touch things, especially natural things like wood and metals and rocks and flowers. And I don't have to see a flower to know if it's real or artificial. I can feel the difference. I had to learn what the world is like through my fingers—the shapes of things and the textures of things. I used to think that the roofs of houses were all flat until I first moved my hands over a model of a town. It was only then that I learned the shape of a church steeple and how streets crisscross a community.

When I was very small, I thought the world was no bigger than the yard around my home in West Roxbury; and my earliest memory is of a swing. I loved the swing because it gave me a feeling of unrestrained motion. A sighted person can see a curtain moving in a breeze, a seagull soaring over a beach, the mailman on his route,

Seeing Without Eyes

the swing of a pendulum on a grandfather clock. As I was not able to see any of these things, I had to create movement. The swing helped me to understand motion in a different way. That is why, even today, I prefer to sit in a rocking chair.

I can remember many things that happened as far back as when I was two years old. People who have been blind since birth often develop very good memories. Perhaps the happiest memories I have of my first two or three years are the stories told to me by my grandmother. She was Irish and truly believed in fairies and leprechauns, and she had lots of stories to tell. Most of the characters she described went around doing good deeds. But there was one villain who crept into many of her stories. His name was Mr. Oooh. He was a terrible creature that had fifty-two million heads and was always trying to drag people down to the bottom of the sea. I was terrified of him, but perhaps not so much as I might have been if I had been able to visualize being dragged to the bottom of the sea.

Sometimes I think a blind child's imagination may be even more vivid than that of a child who can see. I loved the radio serials, especially the Westerns. I have a sort of built-in television screen inside my brain, as do most people. I used to listen to the Lone Ranger tracking down Big Bad Bart and to the story of Huck Finn sailing down the Mississippi. Then I would tune in my BTV (brain television) and imitate the sounds.

For instance, I discovered that bottle caps made a noise just like the jingle of spurs, and I found a way of tapping my slippers on the floor so that they sounded like a galloping horse. Using two brass curtain rods, I would re-create the sound of men fighting a duel with swords. My world was full of make-believe.

Those days of my early childhood were lonely ones because I had no friends except for my sister, Peggy. I guess my parents thought that I had to be overprotected because of my blindness. Now, I see this was a mistake because I soon learned that handicapped children can get along very well with those who are not.

Peggy was two years older than I was, and she was my constant companion when I was a small boy. My parents insisted that she play with me, and she was often fed up with having to take me for walks. One day, when I had awakened her by jumping on her tummy, she decided to have her revenge. She took me for a walk to a tunnel that went under a railroad overpass, but she told me that the trains traveled through the tunnel and not over it. When we were in the middle of the tunnel, Peggy let go of my hand and shouted, "The train's coming!"

I could hear the distant rumble growing louder each second, and I was convinced that I was standing directly in the path of the train. I flung myself to the ground, waiting for steel wheels to chop off my head. The sound grew louder and louder. The tunnel was filled with the thundering noise and the earth shook like an earthquake as the train passed overhead. I was absolutely safe, of course, because the train was separated from me by a thick wall of concrete; but I had never been so frightened.

Peggy was laughing when she grabbed my hand

Seeing Without Eyes

again. I didn't think it was funny. I was angry and frustrated at my dependence on her, but I stopped waking her up in the morning by jumping on her tummy.

I longed to play with boys my own age, and my father seemed to understand this. He spent as much time as he could with me and taught me many games. Other kids on our street would come to watch our games and soon they wanted to join in. That is how I made my first friends outside of the family.

We played basketball in our backyard. Dad installed a buzzer on the basket, and I was able to aim and shoot by listening to the sound. I wasn't very good to start with, but soon I was able to net the ball quite often.

We played for marbles and, at first, I lost all of mine. Then Dad suggested that I challenge the other boys to play after the sun had gone down. When it was dark, I was much better than the other kids; and that is how I won my marbles back.

When I became friends with the other boys, I became a member of the gang on our street. We called ourselves the Greaton Road Gang, and I was not lonely anymore. The gang taught me how to climb trees and do all the other things that young boys like to do.

Not far from our house there was a high wall. In the winter, snow banked up against the wall. The most exciting thing we did in winter was to walk along the top of that wall and jump into a snowdrift. No one in the gang wanted to be the first to jump in case the snow was not deep enough to break the fall, but they didn't tell me that was the reason. Since I couldn't see how far I had to jump, the gang always invited me to go first, as though they were giving me a special privilege.

One of the fellows would lead me along the wall and turn me toward the snowdrift. Then, since I didn't want the Greaton Road Gang to know I was afraid, I would hold my breath and jump.

I will always remember that first jump. It seemed ages before I hit the snow and tumbled over. Then it was my turn to tell each member to jump. Many years later I was to become a skydiver; but when I think of jumping into space, my mind always goes back to the day I first jumped off that high wall into a snowdrift.

Every summer our family went to the little town of Scituate on Cape Cod. That is where the Spook House was and where I learned to fish and sail and swim. There I made many other friends; and one day, because of my blindness, I was able to save some of my friends from great danger. I will tell that story in the next chapter, and take you with me on an adventure at sea.

Lost in the Fog

"That's enough fishing for today," said old Tom McDonagh as he pulled up the anchor. "Remember, never catch more fish than you can eat or give away. There are enough fish in the sea for everyone's need, but not enough for anyone's greed."

Old Tom loved the sea and sailing, and I learned a lot from him. He taught me how to tell the strength of the wind and how to handle the rudder and the ropes of the sails. I no longer needed his help to bait a hook; and I had learned when to strike, how to let the fish run, and how to keep tension on the fishing line. He always caught more fish than I did, but between us that day we had pulled aboard twenty-two flounder in three hours.

As we sailed back into Scituate Harbor, there was a shout from the pier. Old Tom called back a greeting and then turned to me and said, "Now there's someone I want you to meet. He's the lighthouse keeper, Mr. Moriarty. We'll give him half a dozen of our fish and get acquainted with him."

Mr. Moriarty became my friend that day. He had

been the Minot Lighthouse keeper for forty-two years, and his father and grandfather had been lighthouse keepers before him.

He thanked us for the fish, and then he said, "You must come down to see me, Tommy. I'll show you the lighthouse. Bring a friend if you like."

The next day when Frankie Bakey arrived at my home, I told him about Mr. Moriarty's invitation; and he was eager to go. We rode the tandem bike about five miles down the coast to see Mr. Moriarty.

"Now," said Mr. Moriarty, "are you ready to do some climbing? It's a long way up to the top."

And it was. For the first hundred feet we climbed a metal staircase. Then there was a platform, and we had a short rest to catch our breath.

"Now, you'll have to hold on very tight," warned the lighthouse keeper, "because we are going to climb three ladders."

The first two ladders were very narrow steel ones and the third was made of ropes. I tried not to think of how far I would fall if I lost my grip. When we reached the top, Mr. Moriarty pushed open a trapdoor and we climbed outside, alongside the light. The wind was blowing, and it seemed to me that the lighthouse was swaying. On one side I could feel glass, but on the other side there was a sheer drop three hundred feet to the rocks below. Although I could not see the rocks, I could sense the distance.

Right up there on the ledge Mr. Moriarty explained how, for about two hundred years, the Minot Lighthouse had guided ships past the dangerous offshore reefs and into Scituate Harbor and on to Boston.

"In the old days this light guided the sailing ships up and down the coast. Hundreds of ships have been saved from being wrecked on the rocks," he explained.

"How far does the light shine?" I asked.

"Fifty miles," he said, and I couldn't believe him.

"The light bounces off the clouds at night, so ships beyond the horizon are given plenty of warning."

He explained, too, how each lighthouse along the coast flashes its light at different intervals. So, by checking the timing of the flashes against a mariner's chart, sailors know exactly where they are.

"You must get very lonely," I said.

"I have plenty of time to think," he said laughingly. "But when you are doing an important job and helping to save the lives of people, loneliness is not a high price to pay."

While we were talking, the fog rolled in from the sea. I could feel the dampness on my face. Mr. Moriarty then said we would have to go down the ladders to the first level to sound the foghorn.

While we were climbing down the rope ladder, Mr. Moriarty told us the story of how his grandfather had fallen from this same ladder and had broken his leg. And how, although he was in great pain, he had continued to keep the foghorn going all night by pumping bellows. That was in the days before they had installed an electric foghorn with a timing device which automatically sounds the warning. On the platform above the spiral staircase, Mr. Moriarty led me to the desk and placed my finger on the button.

"Tommy, you can start the foghorn today," he said. "There will be many sailors out there who will thank you for it."

I pressed the button, and the foghorn wailed. Curiously, inside the lighthouse the sound was not loud at all; but I could hear the echoes of the foghorn bouncing off the cliffs and buildings far away.

Before we left him to cycle home, Mr. Moriarty gave Frankie and me a meal of baked beans and mugs of steaming coffee.

I did not know then that a week later I would be the one to thank Mr. Moriarty for his vigil in the lighthouse.

Tommy Healey's father had built for himself a sixteen-foot sailboat, and he allowed Tommy to sail it. One day Tommy invited Frankie and me, and two of the neighborhood girls, Barbara Howard and Eileen Kilgariff, to go out for a day's fishing and to explore the mouth of the North River, about eight miles up the coast. We stocked a picnic hamper with tuna sandwiches, Cokes, and a few candy bars, and set sail out of Scituate Harbor. The sun was shining and there was a good breeze blowing. We turned into choppy water at the mouth of the North River and sailed on a high tide to a sandy beach fringed by reeds and marshes. Tommy had forgotten to bring an anchor, so we had to beach the boat alongside the reeds.

It was a great day for a picnic and a great place for

Lost in the Fog

sea birds. I stopped and listened, trying to distinguish one from another. I had been learning to recognize the different sounds of the different species and could identify many of them for my friends.

We took our picnic hamper and set off down the beach, exploring as we went and looking for a good place to swim. The boys took turns carrying the hamper. We played games and swam and then ate our picnic lunch. Tommy looked at his watch and decided it was time for us to be headed home. We had been gone about three hours.

When we got back to the place where we had left the boat, the tide had gone out and the boat was left high and dry in the mud. That meant that we would have to wait for the incoming tide, but by then it would be dark. That thought didn't worry us much because the boat had lights and Tommy knew the coast well. So, we waited.

But about mid-afternoon, the fog once again swept in from the Atlantic, closing in around us. Now we were in trouble, and our trouble doubled at high tide when the outboard motor failed to start. We would have to rely on sail alone. The situation was getting more and more serious.

As the fog grew thicker, the girls began to cry. Without an anchor we could drift onto the rocks or even out to sea. In fact, we could hear the sea beating against the rocks not far away.

Suddenly, the foghorn sounded. The sound was very faint and I was the first to hear it. My heart leaped.

"Listen," I said, and everyone became very quiet. "I

can guide us home. I can tell exactly where the sound of the foghorn is coming from."

At first Tommy didn't trust me. He thought it would be better if we allowed the boat to drift and to wait for the fog to lift. But the sound of the waves beating against the rocks soon persuaded him to put up the sails.

I handed over the rope of the jib sail to Barbara, and Tommy handled the tiller. Then I went forward to the bow and listened to the foghorn of the Minot Lighthouse. I recognized the sound—a high note and a low note every five seconds. We could hear the sounds of other boats, but my ears were tuned to pick out the one sound that would guide us back to safety.

"More to the left," I shouted to Tommy at the tiller. "Now more to the right." I had not yet learned to use the words "port" and "starboard."

"Oooh—Aaah," wailed the foghorn, and I pictured Mr. Moriarty in the snug quarters of his lighthouse thinking about the sailors who depended on his vigilance.

Suddenly, we hit something. The boat lurched and I grabbed the bow rail just in time to save myself from falling overboard. At first we thought we had hit a rock, but there was no sound of a hull being ripped. I yelled to Tommy to drop the sails; but Barbara, who was an experienced sailor, had instinctively released the jib, which was now flapping.

For a moment we were all frozen with fear. I noticed, though, that there was no longer a splash of water against the bow. We were dead still. But why?

Eileen was crying softly. "We are sinking," she

Lost in the Fog

sobbed. "I know we're sinking."

Tommy pulled up the bottom boards and said that there was no water in the bilge. The hull was obviously still sound. But there had to be something holding us. I crept around the boat feeling with my hands against the outer hull at the water level. Then I found what the trouble was: We had hit a lobster boat buoy and its hawser had become entangled with our outboard motor. We had been so preoccupied with the fog and getting home that we had forgotten to lift the motor when we set sail.

Tom with his favorite uncle.

A moment after realizing what had happened, I was aware of a new danger. A faint throb began to grow louder and louder. It was the noise of a boat's engine, and the boat was bearing straight down on us. The others had not noticed the sound.

I yelled, "All of you shout as loud as you can! There's a boat coming right at us!"

We all screamed out together. The crew of the other boat must have heard us because it suddenly swung away and puttered out of earshot into the fog. But we were still stuck and likely to be run down again any minute because this channel was one of the busy ones.

Tommy felt over the taffrail but could not free the hawser.

"Why don't you dive into the water?" I asked.

"Because it's too dark. I can't see anything," he replied.

"Perhaps I can do it," I said. "I'm quite used to the darkness."

I didn't much like the idea of going into the water myself because there had been reports of sharks in the area. That year the warm Gulf Stream had moved exceptionally far north, and man-eating sharks had been caught in the nets of the fishing boats in the Cape Cod area. But I couldn't stop to worry about that.

I gathered my courage and climbed over the rail of the boat, where I sat on the edge of the hull with my feet braced against the side. I took a deep breath and pushed forward into the water. The water was cold and I expected, at any moment, my legs to be snapped off by a denizen of the deep. Although I never confessed it to anyone, I still had a childish fear of Mr. Oooh and his fifty-two million heads.

I guess I was underwater for about twenty seconds, but it seemed much longer. It was long enough, anyway, for me to release the propeller of the outboard from the hawser. Barbara and Frankie pulled me aboard; and when I had taken up my position on the bow, Tommy hoisted the sails. This time we remembered to lift the motor out of the water.

Once more we were underway, and once again I was navigating by the comforting wail of the foghorn at the Minot Lighthouse. We sailed eight miles down the coast with Tommy swinging the rudder at my direction.

"Left. A little more to the left. Hold her steady. Right. That's fine."

We could not have steered a better course on a compass; and as the foghorn grew louder, I knew that we were nearing home. I had to concentrate so hard that I quite forgot to be afraid. Even Eileen began to find the voyage exciting.

It was Eileen who first spotted the light from the lighthouse. She said it was at first very blurred by the fog, but she came up and joined me at the bow and took over the job of giving directions. Hungry and tired, we pulled alongside the Scituate pier and tied up.

Our parents were waiting for us. They had gotten in touch with the Coast Guard, who were out looking for us. A radio message notified the Coast Guard vessel that we were safely home.

The next day, Frankie and I went back to see Mr. Moriarty at the lighthouse; and he listened in silence as we told him about our adventure. All of us had pooled our pocket money and bought him a gift. It was a London-made pipe. He lit up his new pipe while we were there and told us stories about schooners he had sailed on as a boy and about a pirate ship that was seized off the coast when his grandfather had guarded the lighthouse.

Mr. Moriarty made the history and the adventures of the sea very exciting, and I told him that one day I planned to visit places far away.

"Ah, yes," said Mr. Moriarty, puffing at his pipe. "But like me, you'll always want to come back home. I can always tell when I'm near home, even with my eyes shut."

"How can you do that?" I asked.

"I can smell a thousand Irish stews, even when I am five miles out to sea."

"Next time I'll use my nose instead of my ears," I laughed.

Mr. Moriarty clamped a gnarled hand across my shoulders and said, "Tommy, there are not many sailors with the sharpest eyesight who could have done what you did last night—find home port in a fog without a compass."

Even now, long years and many adventures later, whenever I hear a foghorn, I think of Mr. Moriarty; and I even seem to be able to smell the tobacco burning in his new pipe.

Tucky and Other Friends

Some of my favorite memories take me back to my preschool years. One summer, after I had just gone to bed, I heard a commotion on the road in front of our house in Scituate. I heard a truck drive up and stop. Then I heard Dad shouting my name.

"Come out here, Tommy. I have something to show you," he called.

I heard Mom telling Dad that I was probably asleep, but by this time I had found my slippers and robe and was on my way to the porch.

Dad had one of his bowling friends with him and they were both laughing. I walked into the street and Dad guided me to a metal ramp leading onto the truck.

"Go on, son, get into the truck," said Dad.

I walked up the ramp, and the first thing I felt was the hay on the floor of the truck bed. But I could smell an animal. I reached out my hands and felt a warm, shimmering flank. My hands moved down the back of the animal until I touched a wool covering. I kept moving my hands forward until I reached his silk-soft ears.

"It's a horse!" I shouted.

"Almost right," said Dad. "It's a pony and it's all yours, Tommy."

Since I had never seen a horse, I was puzzled by the blanket covering his body and asked a silly question.

"Why is his shirt hanging out?" I asked.

Dad and his friend roared with laughter before they realized that to a blind ten-year-old, it was not such a funny question. I was too excited to notice.

"I'm going to call him Tucky because his shirt needs tucking in," I said. And Tucky he became from that day on.

I begged to go for a ride at once. Dad put a Western saddle on Tucky's back and led me around the block. Then Tucky was led into our yard and tied up for the night. I was too excited to sleep, so I asked if I could sleep in Peggy's room. There I could smell my new friend and listen to him whinny.

Next morning, the news of Tucky's arrival traveled fast, and all the gang came over to see him. They helped me brush him down and we made a small stable out of the tool shed. Now I was king of the block. None of the other children had a pony, and all of them wanted to go for a ride.

"You've got to look after Tucky," warned my father. "That means you've got to feed him regularly, and you'll have to work out some way to pay for his hay."

I did not know it at the time, but Dad was determined even then to make me independent and to realize, as he put it, "that dollars don't grow on trees."

Tucky and Other Friends

To earn the money for Tucky's food, I started charging my friends a dime for a ride. Any of my friends who could not afford a dime was allowed a ride if he helped me clean the stable. I collected enough dimes to buy Tucky his dinner; but once when he broke loose and ate up a neighbor's garden flowers, I had to pay for those, too.

My father was a practical joker and sometimes drank too much. One evening he borrowed Tucky to go to a meeting of the Scituate Beach Association. The mayor was there and so were all the civic-minded townspeople. Dad arrived late and, having had too much to drink, rode Tucky right into the town hall. The mayor was astonished and banged his gavel and called for order. Dad stood up in the stirrups to dismount. The saddle strap was loose, however, and he slipped slowly under Tucky's belly.

Laughter roared through the crowd, but there were some people at the meeting who didn't think this performance was funny at all. They protested to the police because there was a town ordinance that prohibited the keeping of horses within the municipal boundaries. Next day, when the police came around to our house to tell us that Tucky had to go, Dad telephoned a friend who was the city editor of a Boston newspaper. A reporter and photographer arrived shortly, and the next edition of the newspaper carried a big heartthrob story with pictures about a small blind boy who was going to be deprived of his pony by the heartless city fathers of Scituate.

Many people wrote letters to the editor, and others held meetings to defend Tucky's right to stay in the town. As there was a town election coming up, the city fathers changed their minds and allowed Tucky to stay. But Tucky had to behave in such a way as to prove he had earned the privilege of being the only pony in Scituate. His chance came on Labor Day. Dad and I had entered him in the Labor Day parade. Dad had bought a small cart, and Tucky, festooned with ribbons, proudly pulled the cart loaded with four crippled children.

The parade marked the end of the summer vacation, and the question was raised as to what to do with Tucky when we returned to West Roxbury. I hated the thought of leaving him behind. Suddenly an idea occurred to me.

"I know what to do," I told Dad. "Let's give Tucky and the pony cart to the home for crippled children."

And that is what we did. For many years, and until he was sent to a ranch in his old age, Tucky and his cart gave great joy to many children who had lost the use of their legs.

Back in West Roxbury, I missed Tucky; but there I had another gang of friends—the Greaton Road Gang. I had grown to love animals, and one of the things we did as a gang was to collect stray or injured cats and dogs. We would house them in my family's garage until we found the owners. We started in a small way, but the garage soon became a miniature zoo.

My closest friend, Billy Hannon, brought in birds with broken wings; and we built special cages for them so that they would not be eaten by the cats. Because my

Tucky and Other Friends

sense of touch was highly developed, I was often able to find out what was wrong with the birds and other animals more easily than my friends who could see.

I would tell Billy, "This bird has a broken wing. I can feel the bone." Then between us we would gently bind the wing to the side of the bird and give the wing time to mend. Not all of the animals recovered from our first aid, but most of them did.

At one time the garage contained eighteen cats, four dogs, six birds, two squirrels, five turtles, a snake, and a monkey that Dad had brought from Venezuela. The animals often made a terrible noise at night, especially the cats, and the odor wasn't improving any. Once again the townspeople complained.

This time a newspaper story about "a little blind boy's animal sanctuary" did not help to prevent the authorities from closing down my homemade zoo.

Mom and Dad did allow me to keep one dog, called Pal. He was a real delinquent and often sneaked down to the delicatessen on the corner. He would steal bologna sausages, knock ice-cream cones out of the hands of small children, and knock over garbage cans. One day when Dad was in the delicatessen, the owner chased Pal outside and said to Dad, "If I ever find the owner of that dog, I'll sue him for a fortune."

After that I had to keep Pal in our yard.

During those years, Dad owned a nightclub in an old four-story building. Only the first two floors were used for the club, and our Greaton Road Gang was allowed to use the upper floors to play. We made them our gang headquarters and built our own gym there. In bad weather it was there that we played basketball. We set up a boxing ring and Tussey Russell, a retired professional middleweight contender, taught us how to box. Of course, I was the most popular opponent among my friends because I could never see a straight left to my chin.

I boxed by flailing my arms like the sails of a windmill. I guess I looked a lot more dangerous than I was. One day, though, I did manage to hit Tussy Russell. I think the old fellow must have been looking the other way and was caught off balance. Anyway, Tussey hit the canvas; and I was given a cheer because no other member of the Greaton Road Gang had been able to knock him down.

Of course, it was not all holidays for me. Like every other boy I went to school—not to the neighborhood school with Billy and my other friends, but to a special school for the blind.

One day, a few years earlier, I had come in from playing to find a lady, Miss Kelly, waiting to see me. I did not know who Miss Kelly was, but she asked me to sit at the dining table and play a game with her. I didn't want to play because I had a boil on my buttock, which hurt when I sat down. But I sat because my parents were insistent.

Miss Kelly produced about twenty small wooden blocks and invited me to make squares, circles, and triangles. This seemed a tame and silly game; but because the boil was hurting, I made the shapes as quickly as possible. Then Miss Kelly recited about a dozen numbers and asked me to repeat them, first forward and then backward. I did not find that game difficult either.

As I was only six years old at the time, I did not understand that Miss Kelly was giving me an IQ test. When she had finished the tests, I overheard her telling my mother that my scores were that of a genius. I thought a genius was probably a friend of the genie that appeared when Aladdin rubbed his magic lamp.

Anyway, my doing well on the IQ tests resulted in my being placed in an advanced class at the Perkins School for the Blind in Watertown, Massachusetts. It is a famous school; and the best known of the students who have gone there is Helen Keller, who was both deaf and blind.

Like every other child, I didn't want to go to school. If I had known that Miss Kelly's "games" were a sort of entrance examination, I am sure I would have flunked every test on purpose.

After Miss Kelly had left, Dad said he would cure my boil with an old Irish remedy he had learned from his grandmother. He filled a bottle with boiling water, sealing off the neck with a square of tinfoil. Then, turning me upside down across his knee, he placed the top of the bottle over the boil and slipped the tinfoil out. My screams were heard by Billy down the street. But, curiously enough, I have never had another boil, so I guess the painful Irish remedy worked.

"Never mind," said Dad when I had stopped screaming. "I've got a surprise for you. You are going to a special school where they will teach you how to read with your fingers and to play special games invented for blind children."

I started to protest again. "I don't want to learn to read. I can listen to the stories on the radio and to the ones Grandma tells. I like the games I play with Billy and the Turnbull twins."

"You can come home every weekend," Dad said, reassuringly.

But that was the worst thing he could have said because until then I had not understood that I would actually have to leave home and stay in a strange room.

That night I cried myself to sleep; but all my tears did not stop my parents' plan to send me away to the Perkins School, where I was to discover a whole new world.

Learning to Live

That first day at school is one I should like to forget.

"Here we are," said Mom as the car turned into the gates of the Perkins School for the Blind. "Isn't it exciting?"

It was awful! Twenty small blind children were being torn from their parents and from their homes for the first time. I wanted to run away. But where could I run to? I didn't even know where I was.

I survived those first torturous hours, however, and was given a bedroom which I was to share with another blind boy, Billy Nicholson. He was even more miserable than I was, if such a thing was possible. I tried to get him to stop crying by teaching him to do somersaults. Then the housemother, Miss Harrison, came in and said it was time to stop playing and to go to sleep. But I could not go to sleep. I was thinking of Pal and the Greaton Road Gang, and I wanted my Mom to come and say goodnight to me.

I was just beginning to get sleepy when I smelled something burning. It smelled like the odor of Dad's cigar when he stumped it out in an ashtray. I knew that Billy would not be smoking cigars, so I got out of bed and followed the smell to a ventilator shaft. I put my ear against the ventilator and heard a faint crackling sound.

The cause of both the crackling sound and the smell of smoke suddenly dawned on me. I grabbed Billy by the shoulders and shook him awake.

"Let's get out of here!" I said. "There's something burning! We must tell Miss Harrison."

Billy didn't seem to understand. But I knew I had to do something quickly. My first problem was to find the door in this strange room. I clicked my tongue on the roof of my mouth. The echo bounced off three walls, and the sound was absorbed by the draperies on the fourth wall. The door had to be opposite the window, I figured. I found the door and ran down the hall, calling Miss Harrison. A moment later she came running down the hallway.

"Why aren't you in bed?" she asked.

"Fire!" I said. "There's something burning!"

Miss Harrison sniffed. "Don't be silly, Tommy. I can't smell anything."

I led her back into the bedroom. "It's over there," I protested and pushed her toward the ventilator shaft. "Can't you hear something crackling?"

"You've been dreaming," said Miss Harrison. "Now you go back to sleep."

But I was frantic and shouted, "I can smell it! I can hear it!"

Miss Harrison paused. She had been a housemother

of blind children for a long time, and she knew that a blind child's senses of hearing and smell were often more acute than those of sighted people. She sniffed again.

"You're right, Tommy. There *is* something burning."

She ordered Billy and me to get out into the hall at once. I heard her running to the other bedrooms to awaken all the children in the dormitory. When we were all in the hall, she told us to line up and hold onto the pajamas of the child in front of us. Then we snaked our way outside. Miss Harrison telephoned the janitor and sounded the fire alarm.

We learned later that it had been a very small fire that was easily extinguished by a fire extinguisher. A fuse box in the cellar had short-circuited, and the wood frame around the box had started to smolder. If the fire had not been detected early, the whole dormitory might have burned. It could have been very serious.

I suppose that to a blind person, nothing is more frightening than a fire; but one advantage of being blind is that one is apt to smell danger quickly. I was beginning to realize how important my senses of smell and hearing were.

The next day I found myself in a class with six other children, including two girls. The boy next to me introduced himself as Ernie Anderson. He produced an apple from his pocket and asked me if I wanted a bite. That was the beginning of a friendship that was to last throughout my school days. Jerry Pierce, another boy in the class, also became a close friend. We did everything together and called ourselves the "Three Musketeers."

Adventures in Darkness

We were always looking for adventure and were constantly getting into trouble.

After the first week of school, Jerry, Ernie, and I decided to run away. We had discovered a hole in the fence and decided it would be worth a try. Climbing through the hole, we found ourselves on a grassy bank. Just ahead of us was the sound of running water. We did not know that the running water was the Charles River. Years later I was to receive glory on the Charles River as a rower; but that day, Ernie slipped on a rock and fell into the water. Although the water was quite shallow, he could not get out because the bank was so muddy. He kept slipping back in. I took off my belt, handed him one end, and pulled on the other. He finally made it. Wet and miserable, we made our way back to the hole in the fence. Our first attempt at running away was not very successful.

While I did not fully appreciate it at the time, I began to learn lessons that would help me live a full and exciting life. The most important of the early lessons was how to read.

A sighted child learns his alphabet and simple words by looking at the print, but a blind child learns to read with his fingers. He uses a system known as Braille, named for Louis Braille, who invented the system more than a hundred years ago. Each letter of the Braille alphabet and each number is transcribed into raised dots on paper.

The letter "B," for instance, is written in raised dots in this formation : and the number eight is written :. and so on. The Braille alphabet and the numerals are shown on page 50. To speed up a blind person's reading, a system has been devised for combining dots to spell out commonly used words like "the" and "love."

Of course, fingertips do not read as quickly as eyes; so a Braille reader takes more time to read a book. Today, the cassette recorder is used by blind people much more than is Braille. Sighted people read books into tape recorders; and the result is that blind people have whole libraries of taped books, ranging from the latest novels to the most technical scientific textbooks and journals.

But when I started school, the modern cassette-type recorder had not yet been invented. Braille was very important to me, and it still is. For instance, when I want to take down a telephone number or make a note, I use Braille.

Once I had learned how to read and write in Braille, I had fun teaching the system to my sighted friends, including Billy Hannon and the Turnbull twins. They used it as a secret code, which their parents and teachers could not read.

It is not hard to learn to write or read Braille. Take a piece of thick paper and a sharp pencil and punch the pencil into the paper so that a raised dot is made on the underside of the paper. It is easier to make dots if the paper is placed on top of cardboard. When you punch the dots, you must start on the right side of the paper and work to the left so that when you turn the paper over, your fingers will read from left to right, in the same way as you would read print.

Of course, if you want to write Braille properly, you can get a special slate and a pointed instrument called a stylus at one of the many Braille institutes. It is fascinating to discover that your fingers can become your eyes, and that you can even read in the dark.

Braille is truly an international form of communication. Those small impressions on paper have opened up a new world for blind people like me. The system is always being improved, and now there are special kinds of typewriters and printing presses that turn out Braille impressions very rapidly.

I learned to read and write just as quickly as sighted children do, and soon I was reading the adventures of Jim Hawkins in *Treasure Island,* and living the adventures of Tom Sawyer when he sailed down the Mississippi.

I took my Braille books to bed at night; and when all the kids were supposed to be asleep, I was able to go on reading my favorite adventure stories. It saves on electricity, too.

The story I loved best at that age was about a black Arabian stallion that was trained by a boy of my age and which became the greatest racehorse in America. I imagined myself to be the boy in the story. I practiced making the noise of thundering hooves and pretended that I was riding the black stallion to victory.

I learned mathematics by using an abacus, the most ancient form of the adding machine. The Chinese invented the abacus several thousand years ago. Basically, it is a small board with rows of beads or counters that can be moved up and down on rods. A counter on the lowest

Learning to Live

line signifies one, on the next line ten, on the next one hundred, and so on. When the beads are moved up and down the rods, it becomes quite easy to add, substract, and divide. The abacus was really the first computer.

In our special class I was constantly being taught how to learn through my fingers. I was creating mental images by feeling things. Geography was exciting. Instead of an ordinary atlas, my atlas had many impressions to mark oceans, land areas, rivers, and mountains. For instance, the oceans were indicated by raised lines. I learned the different shapes of the states in the United States with a jigsaw puzzle. By fitting the different pieces of the puzzle, I soon discovered that Texas was the biggest state and Rhode Island was the smallest. Since then, of course, we've added Alaska, which is now the largest. I learned that Colorado joined with Wyoming, Nebraska, Kansas, a small strip of Oklahoma, New Mexico, the northeast corner of Arizona, and Utah. I discovered that Florida was shaped like a frying pan.

My fingers relayed these sensory messages to my brain and locked them in my memory in the same way that sighted children record images through their eyes.

Some of our most exciting lessons were learned on field trips. We would go by bus to the Boston Museum of Science and Industry, where I first discovered the size and shape of a tiger. It was a stuffed tiger, of course, but I put my hand inside its mouth and felt its huge teeth. After that, I could easily understand why people were frightened by tigers. I discovered, too, the huge spread of an eagle's wings and how the bird was able to support itself in flight. I learned the principles of aerodynamics and the different kinds of aircraft.

My hands were eager to reach out for everything, even simple things like Inca pottery. Handling the tools and artifacts of ancient man made history become alive and interesting to me. I wanted to know more about ancient civilizations and the way of life in foreign lands.

When it came time to return to Perkins, Tom's sadness at leaving was mixed with the excitement of seeing his friends again.

Learning to Live

One of the most important lessons I learned at Perkins was mobility—how to find my way around, not only on the campus, but in the everyday world.

Every blind person wants to be as independent as a sighted person and able to lead a normal life. My first lesson in mobility was how to use a white cane. Most people, at one time or another, have seen a blind person walking, swinging his cane from side to side. The cane helps him to discover obstacles in his path before he bumps into them or trips over them—the curb of a sidewalk, furniture, light posts, or things like that.

When you see a person with a white cane, you should not be nervous about asking if he needs help to find direction or to cross a street. But don't assume that every blind person needs help. Some of them enjoy the challenge of finding their way on their own and are perfectly capable of doing so.

What too often happens is that a sighted person with good intentions will just grab the arm of a blind person and pull him across the street. But the blind person might not want to cross the street. Always ask first. Then, if the blind person takes advantage of your offer, allow him to hold on to your arm, never hold on to him. If you are holding a blind person by the elbow, then he is really guiding you.

My mobility teacher, Mrs. Cathy Riley, was puzzled at how easily I managed to get around without using a cane. She watched me walk along a sidewalk without bumping into people, a wall, or a telegraph pole.

"Can you see at all?" she asked.

"I can see nothing," I answered.

"Can you tell light from darkness?" asked Mrs. Riley.

"I don't know what you mean by 'light'," I replied.

"Then how do you manage to avoid obstacles?" she asked.

I thought about that for a moment and then said, "I sort of see with my cheeks."

Mrs. Riley was very interested to discover that I have "facial vision" (which I mentioned earlier). I believe that this built-in radar system can be developed by everyone. You could experiment to find out if you can "see" in the dark. Shut your eyes and walk through your house making clicking noises with your tongue every two or three seconds. It may be difficult at first, but soon your ears will pick up the echoes, and you will know where the walls are and be able to locate, say an open door in a room. It would be useful to use this echo method to find your way on a very dark night.

Because I have been blind since birth, my own radar is supersensitive. In fact, I can avoid most obstacles without making a clicking sound. The airwaves caused by my movement bounce off obstacles and hit my cheeks. This radar system, however, is not foolproof. It does not always work for me; and I have bumped into more things than I can count, especially when running. I have often knocked myself out and have even ended up with concussions. That's easy to do when you run into a concrete pillar!

Scientists have recently invented a cane that is elec-

Learning to Live

trically wired to send out "beeps." The beeps echo back from obstacles, warning a blind person of danger. I was one of the first to test the beeping cane, but I found my facial vision to be more reliable.

The science of learning mobility has been given the name parapetology. I am sure that in time there will be many more inventions to help blind people function in a sighted world without assistance. But so far, no one has discovered anything more useful than a seeing-eye dog. Later, I shall introduce you to Heidi, my own seeing-eye dog, and explain how she helps me to navigate not only around my own town, but even in distant countries.

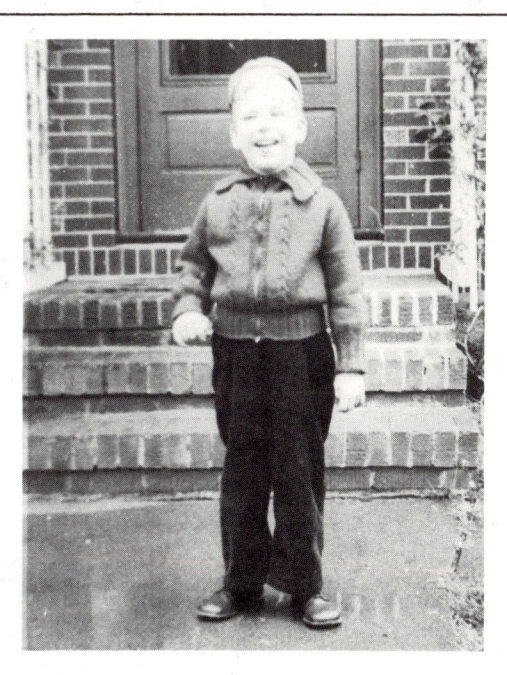

Early childhood for Tom was filled with playing outdoors.

Braille Alphabet and Numerals

The six dots of the Braille cell are arranged and numbered this way:

1 • • 4
2 • • 5
3 • • 6

A blind person reads by running his fingers over the raised dots that make up the Braille alphabet. Tom usually signs his name in Braille, and his signature is printed underneath the dedication in the front of this book.

How to Play the Game

One thing I could not do with the Greaton Road Gang was play baseball. Most of the gang were members of a Little League team; and when they went off to play on Saturday mornings, they left me behind. And I was miserable.

Dad knew just how miserable, and one day he came home from work with a baseball bat he had made himself.

"Okay, Tommy, I'm going to teach you to play baseball," he said. "We'll go practice in the backyard."

Instead of a baseball, however, he began by pitching a basketball at me and shouting, "Here it comes. Hit it, son."

Of course, I could not gauge the ball's speed nor see its approach. I would miss every time and get angry at myself.

"Well, let's try it a different way," Dad suggested. "I'll roll the ball along the ground, and that way you'll hear it coming."

I listened intently and heard the scrunch of the ball

on the gravel. When I guessed the ball was at my feet, I lashed out. But I hit only about one ball out of twenty.

"It's just no good," I cried. "I'll never learn how to hit the ball."

"Hold on a minute," said Dad. "I've got another idea. I'm going to throw the ball so that it will bounce six feet in front of you. As soon as you hear the bounce, swing your bat."

I waited for the sound of the bounce and then swung the bat. It was a perfect connection, and the sound was music to my ears. I was very excited. I did not hit every ball that was bounced in front of my feet, but soon I was hitting most of them.

That day, when the boys came back from their Little League game, they discovered I had a game of my own and wanted to join in. Of course, it was not proper baseball. Dad called it the Sullivan Rules Game. Soon the Greaton Road Gang seemed to prefer the Sullivan Rules Game to their Little League game. By using my ears instead of my eyes, I was able to hit the ball almost as well as Tommy Healey, Frankie Bakey, and the others.

But I still wanted to play real baseball, and I kept nagging the gang to let me play. I thought I might be better at pitching than batting, so Frankie volunteered to be my catcher. He pounded his fist in the catcher's glove behind the plate and I pitched in the direction of the sound. At first, I threw wildly, often missing the plate by yards; but slowly, with Frankie's directions and corrections, I got better and better. I was becoming fairly accurate.

How to Play the Game

Then the day came when the gang invited me to play in one of their Little League games. A number of parents showed up to see the "little blind boy" play baseball. The game started and I was given the ball. Frankie pounded his glove and I threw the ball with all my strength. A scream of pain erupted. My ball had hit the batter in the face and loosened his two front teeth. It was a disaster! The parents of the injured player objected and said they would not allow their son to play in the Little League unless I was forbidden to play.

That was my first and last game of real baseball. I was really quite bitter, even though the Greaton Road Gang still liked to play the Sullivan Rules Game.

I longed to participate in sports more than anything else. I began secretly to hate boys who could see; they could catch and hit balls. I listened to all the sports commentaries on the radio and soon knew the names of all the top league players in baseball, football, basketball and hockey. I was an avid fan. Even though I couldn't play, I could keep up with what was going on—as a vicarious participant.

At the Perkins School I started to invent games that I could participate in. For instance, in the dormitory we played what we called Perkins' hockey. Two players would squat ten yards apart in a corridor and slide a slipper along the floor. The object was to get the slipper past the other player's legs. The game was fun, but it was still too tame a game for me.

One day, after listening to a game of tennis on the radio, I worked out a game of Sullivan Rules Tennis.

Well, it wasn't exactly tennis, but it was the next best thing.

We had a running track at the school. To keep the blind runners on the track, a guide wire was stretched at shoulder height from the starting point to the finish. A ring about the size of a Frisbee was put around this wire,

Mr. Sullivan, like all dads, was very proud of his son.

and the blind competitor held the ring as he ran. I was not much good at running, and I didn't take much interest in the track. That's how my Sullivan Rules Tennis originated. I invented a game in which two players with bats tried to hit the ring back and forth to each other along the wire. As the ring bounced along the wire, it made a metallic sound. Soon we became skilled at judging when the ring was approaching, and we would then swipe it back.

And about that time I learned how to bowl, too. We had a rail leading to the bowling alley. By sliding a hand along the rail, we learned when and in what direction to roll the ball. It was great to hear the sound of falling pins. A signal was used to let us know when the pins were in place again.

Other sports at Perkins included high jumping and broad jumping, but always with special rules because we were blind. In high jumping, instead of running toward the bar, we were allowed to take only one step before leaping. Not being able to see the bar made it essential to be very accurate. Before I left Perkins, in my late teens, I managed to clear five feet. At that time five feet was a record for a blind athlete.

But I continued to yearn to compete against boys who were not blind. I was growing tall and strong; and I knew that if I could find one sport in which sight did not matter, I could test my skill and strength against anybody. If I could not see, how could I play football or baseball or hockey?

Sometimes I would shout at Mom and Dad, "Why

can't I see? Why can't I be like Frankie and Tommy Healey? The thing I want most to do in the world, I'll never be able to do. I'll never be any good at any sport except the Sullivan Rules Games."

"You'll just have to accept your blindness and make the best of it," said Mom quietly.

"I won't! I won't!" I yelled and ran upstairs to my bedroom, where I buried my head in a pillow and screamed with anger.

But one day at school, the whole world changed for me. It was on a Tuesday. After classes were over, a man called Mr. Dick Kamus invited all the boys to go to the gymnasium. Ernie, Jerry, and I wondered why he wanted to see us. When we reached the gym, Mr. Kamus made us stand in a circle around him. Then he took each one of us separately by the shoulders and pushed us to the floor. We were surprised and angry.

The only people who had a right to push me over, I argued, were my friends when we had a fight. I picked myself up from the floor and used a swear word I had heard my Dad use. Mr. Kamus laughed. That made me angrier still. I bent my head forward and charged in the direction of the laughter. I butted Mr. Kamus in his stomach. That stopped his laughter. Then he said, "I wanted to see how each of you would react to being pushed over. You are all angry with me, aren't you? Especially Tommy. I want to teach you a sport in which you will have many falls. But you must learn to control your tempers. It is one of the oldest sports in the world. It is called wrestling."

How to Play the Game

Rubbing my bruised elbow where I had fallen, I said, "I don't want to learn anything from you."

"Why are you still angry?" asked Mr. Kamus.

"Because you hurt me, and I want to hurt you," I protested.

"In wrestling you will learn to fall without getting hurt," said Mr. Kamus.

"It's just another special game for blind kids," I said, still furious at Mr. Kamus and even more furious at being blind.

"No, you're wrong," said Mr. Kamus. "In wrestling you will be able to compete against people who can see. It's what we call a body-contact sport, and there is no reason why each one of you couldn't become a champion wrestler—not only the best at Perkins, but in Massachusetts. Perhaps one of you might become the best wrestler in your weight class in America."

My heart began to beat faster. Was this the sport I had been waiting to discover? Was this the one chance to compete on equal terms with other boys, even though I could not see?

So it was that Mr. Kamus began to teach us the fine art of wrestling. I soon learned that this sport is not just a matter of trying to grab your opponent and knock him over with sheer strength. There are strict rules and many different holds. It is a sport that requires skill, but not necessarily sight.

A match comprises three periods of three minutes each. In the first period, both contenders stand up; and the object is to throw your opponent off his feet. In the second and third periods, the contenders are in a kneeling position; and the aim is to "pin" one's opponent on his back on the floor. There are illegal holds that cost penalties and there are rules for scoring, but I am not going to describe wrestling in detail in this book. It would take too long. There are many books on wrestling and many schools that have wrestling classes, and I have other stories to tell.

I soon discovered that wrestling was indeed a sport that seemed to have been invented especially for me. It didn't matter that I could not see. I could feel my opponent. I could train, strengthen my muscles, and speed up my reaction time.

My anger over being blind and my frustrations were channeled into a desire to excel in a sport in which I could take part on terms of equality with boys who had vision. It was a maturing process, both physically and emotionally.

Every day I went to the gym at Perkins to be coached by Mr. Kamus. I practiced until my muscles ached. I practiced until the sweat poured off me. And I was exhilarated by the challenge. Now I had a goal. I was determined to be the best wrestler in my weight class.

I was selected for the Perkins School wrestling team. At fourteen, I was the team's youngest member. In my first match, I was paired to wrestle against a boy who was not blind. I had the kind of feeling one gets before going to the dentist. In the locker room, where I changed into my school uniform, my fingers trembled so much that I could hardly lace my shoes. My parents had come from

How to Play the Game 59

School friends are important to all youngsters, and Tom had a lot of fun with his friends.

West Roxbury to see my first match, and the bleachers in the gymnasium were filled with supporters from both Perkins and the visiting rival school.

Then I heard my name called. My legs felt as if they were made of rubber as I walked from the locker room into the gymnasium and to the mat where my opponent was waiting. I had expected to hear a round of applause and the usual cheer of encouragement from my schoolmates. Instead, a wave of laughter greeted my arrival. I could not understand it. Above the laughter Mr. Kamus shouted, "Your uniform is inside out."

What had happened in the locker room was that, in my nervousness, I had put on my tights and pants with the school colors against my goose-pimpled flesh. The fluffy white lining of the uniform was on the outside. I must have looked like an Easter bunny. Worst of all, there was a label dangling from the seat of my pants. The label read, "Machine wash, warm—tumble dry."

When I realized that everyone was laughing at me, I turned from the mat to run back to the locker room. Then Mr. Kamus hissed in my ear, "Are you quitting, Tommy? I thought you had more guts."

In some ways the next three seconds were among the most important in my life. If I had run back to the locker room with the laughter still ringing in my ears, I don't think I would ever have wrestled again. Mr. Kamus would have taken no further interest in me. I turned toward my sighted opponent, and the referee blew his whistle for the match to begin.

Half a minute later the match was over. I was thrashed.

But I had won a much more important victory that day. Afterward Mr. Kamus put his arm around my shoulders and congratulated me.

"But I lost," I protested.

How to Play the Game

Then Mr. Kamus quoted the famous lines of the poet Grantland Rice:

For when the One Great Scorer comes
To write against your name,
He marks—not that you won or lost—
But how you played the game.

I was not sure, at the time, what Mr. Kamus meant because I was still thinking of what a fool I had made of myself. But, of course, later on I understood.

From then on Mr. Kamus took a special interest in me, and he gave me extra coaching. I lost my next six wrestling matches, but not my determination. Before my seventh match, Mr. Kamus told me that I should not expect to win it—that I didn't have a chance.

"Your opponent is three years older than you are, Tommy," he warned, "and he has never lost a match. But learn as much as you can from him."

Because Mr. Kamus expected me to lose, I had no prematch jitters. I was quite relaxed when I went to the mat. No one was more surprised than I when I "took down" my challenger in the first period. He equaled the points in the second period with a "reversal." In the third period "I escaped" and so marked up my first victory by a score of three to two.

I did not lose again in 384 consecutive wrestling matches—a record that led me to the U.S. national title and an invitation to participate in the Olympic trials.

Wrestling did much more for me than build up my muscles and sinews and teach me physical coordination. One of the key lessons I learned was that although handicapped, I could make my way in a world of sighted people. I also learned that I was not just wrestling for my own glory, but for my team. I learned discipline. Whether I wanted to or not, I knew that if I was to keep my body and mind in top form, I had to train every day.

When, at the age of seventeen, I won a national title, a strange thing happened to me. I went off by myself and cried. I was miserable because I had achieved my goal. I thought that I could not go any further, and I felt drained and empty inside.

How wrong I was! A national wrestling title was just one of many goals I was to set and reach. As I went along I would find out what these goals would be. I would strain and strive until I reached them.

Anyway, I was still to discover the most rewarding part of wrestling. This I found when I, too, became a coach. I am always looking for other Tommy Sullivans, who may lose their first few matches and who may even put their uniforms on inside out. I not only want to teach them how to be good wrestlers but to pass along to them the philosophy that Mr. Kamus taught me—that what counts most is not whether you win or lose, but how you play the game.

And what I'm really talking about now is the game of life.

The Dream of Tomorrow

At Perkins, Ernie, Jerry, and I were always getting into trouble. Every day at recess we would meet to decide our next adventure or our next escapade, as the case might be. One day we picked on Jimmy. Jimmy, one of the boys in our class, would do almost anything we told him to do—things that we would not have dared to do, like putting a snake in the housemother's bed or playing "Jingle Bells" on the school chimes.

We liked Jimmy, but we often took advantage of him because he was so gullible. One day we talked Jimmy into putting on a small suit of armor that was exhibited in the school museum. It was early in the morning, just before assembly, which was held in the school chapel.

"Now, Jimmy," we said, "when you hear the bell for assembly, you walk into the chapel with your armor on."

"Okay," replied Jimmy cheerfully from behind the visor of the armor.

Ernie, Jerry, and I hurried on ahead to the chapel

and took our seats. The school principal had started distributing the program for the day when we heard Jimmy arrive. He sounded like a dozen garbage cans being clanged together. The clatter grew louder and louder as Jimmy, encased in the armor, started to walk down the marble aisle. The three of us stuffed handkerchiefs into our mouths to keep from laughing and almost choked from the effort. Just as Jimmy reached the center aisle, he tripped and fell. The noise was deafening. The principal stopped speaking in the middle of a sentence to investigate the commotion. Since we didn't want Jimmy to get into trouble on our account, we confessed that the whole prank had been our idea.

The principal was furious and his voice registered his anger.

"You three boys are the worst-behaved in the whole school," he told us. "You are just going to have to learn the hard way. All three of you will have to stay at school this weekend. I'm going to call your parents and notify them at once."

The three of us always went home on weekends. Our parents would come for us on Friday afternoon and return us to school on Sunday night. We felt that the punishment was unfair. After all, we argued, nobody had been hurt by having Jimmy borrow the museum's suit of armor.

We sulked all afternoon.

"Let's run away," I said.

"Where can we run to?" asked Jerry.

"Yeah, we can't go home because our parents will

The Dream of Tomorrow

just bring us back to school again," reflected Ernie, who was always the practical one.

I thought about the problem for a moment and then suggested, "We can sail down the river just like Huck Finn did."

"But we haven't got a raft," protested Ernie, "and how can we find our way?"

"We'll take one of the school's rowboats and just let it drift down the river," I replied. "The river runs to the sea, and we might just drift to a tropical island or some other exciting place. Anyway, it's worth giving it a try."

"Anything is better than staying at school through the weekend," added Jerry.

During the next three days we took food from the dining room—chicken legs, bread, peanut butter, and anything else we could save from our plates. We pooled our money and found we had six dollars and thirty-nine cents among us—not very much for a journey into the unknown and the unseen.

Every night when we went to bed, Jerry, Ernie, and I would take turns listening at the window for the night watchman on his rounds. We wanted to find out at what time he would be farthest away from our dorm. We also listened for the cars of teachers arriving and departing. We wanted to make sure that we would not be caught at the school gate.

Then on Friday night, when most of the other students had gone home for the weekend, the "Three Musketeers" put their escape plan into action.

A church clock sounded eleven. Jerry was at the

window. He reported that the night watchman had just passed on the pavement below. The housemother had gone to her room, and the coast was clear. We dressed quickly, stored all the food in Ernie's Scout knapsack, and prepared to depart.

"Okay," I whispered, "let's go."

"Who said you're the leader?" asked Jerry.

"It was my idea," I answered.

"That's right," agreed Ernie. "Tommy is the captain, but he'd better be a good one or we'll mutiny."

We had already made our plans. Just outside the window at the end of the hall was a drainpipe. It was a bit rickety, but we felt confident that it would bear our weight if we climbed down one at a time. If the pipe were to give way, we would fall fifteen feet onto the concrete below. As I was the leader, I had to test the strength of the pipe. With my fingertips I felt the rough surface of the bricks, and then my hand touched the metal of the pipe.

I took a firm grip and then let my feet slip from the windowsill. The pipe rattled threateningly, and I thought it was going to pull away from the wall. I tried not to think of how far I could fall. Fortunately, the pipe held. My arms were strong from climbing ropes in the gym, and I slowly let myself down until I reached the sidewalk below.

"Okay, you guys," I whispered, "come on."

Ernie and Jerry followed without mishap.

We were familiar with the layout of the campus, and it was not difficult for us to find our way to the main gate. But as we arrived there, we heard a car coming. It was probably one of the teachers returning late. We hid behind a bush and remained absolutely still. Of course, we could not see the lights of the car, but we knew that the driver might see us. The car passed on and we knew we were safe; we walked through the gate.

Now we had to turn right, onto the road that led to the school's boathouse on the Charles River. If a policeman had seen us, he certainly would have stopped us. He would have known that three boys with white canes had to be from the Perkins School. But the street was empty except for a couple of stray cats playing around a garbage can.

Soon we heard the sound of water lapping at the dock leading from the boathouse. The door of the boathouse was locked, but we found a window at the back. Ernie slipped the blade of his Scout knife into a crack in the window frame and lifted the latch. Then we climbed into the boathouse. We unlocked the door from the inside. After much heaving and pushing, we managed to get a small rowboat into the water. Ernie went back for the oars. We pulled away from the dock and rowed into midstream, guided by the sound of water lapping along the banks. Then we shipped the oars and allowed the rowboat to drift.

The night was very quiet, except for occasional cars on the road that ran parallel with the river. We guessed we were moving at the same speed as the current, which was about two knots. We were far too excited to be afraid.

Suddenly, we heard the sound of music and someone singing.

"It must be someone with a radio," said Jerry.

"No," replied Ernie, "it's someone playing a guitar."

At first we thought that the singer was in another boat, but then we realized that the voice came from the bank of the river.

"Let's investigate," I said. "It can't be a cop. Cops don't sing."

Jerry and I pulled on the oars and rowed in the direction of the music. Just as the boat hit the mud at the bank, a friendly voice called out to us. "Hey, what are you guys up to?"

"Just rowing," I answered cautiously.

"Like some coffee?" asked the singer.

"Sure," we chorused.

In getting out of the boat, I stepped into a mudhole. The singer came down and helped us onto the grassy bank. "Wow!" he said. "You sure are clumsy. Are you blind or something?"

"Yes, we all are," I said. "We've run away from Perkins School."

As we shared a mug of hot coffee, the singer listened without interrupting as we told our story and how we planned to row right out to sea. Then he roared with laughter.

"You're the craziest kids I've ever come across," he said. "But perhaps it's the crazy people who are really the most intelligent, or the most interesting anyway." The singer then told us his name, Peter Whitney, and how he, too, had run away from college and from his home. He said his father wanted him to go into his business, but that he did not want to join what he called the "rat race."

"There are more important things than making money," he said.

"Like what?" asked Jerry.

"Like meeting crazy kids like you," he laughed.

He told us how he had wandered from town to town, playing and singing at clubs and earning enough to eat, and usually enough to pay for a place to sleep. He described himself as a wandering minstrel and explained how, in the old days in Europe, the wandering minstrels did exactly what he was doing. He said that his music had allowed him to travel all over Europe, and now he was planning to work his way back to California. He was considering returning to school because he was a bit older and a great deal wiser than when he had left.

Although Peter was only twenty years old, he seemed as wise as a professor; and his adventures sounded more exciting than any I had ever heard. We shared our chicken and our peanut butter sandwiches with him.

Peter talked to us as though we were adults and not just kids. Then he asked, "How are you going to get past the locks at Brighton?"

"Oh, we'll think of something," I said nonchalantly.

"I'd like to come with you, but they would probably arrest me for contributing to the misdemeanor of juveniles."

We were not sure what he meant by that. He helped us push the boat into the river again and, as we said good-bye to the wandering minstrel, he shouted, "Good luck. Hold on to your dreams."

The wandering minstrel was right in assuming that we would have trouble when we reached the locks at Brighton. By the time we arrived at the locks, the sun was up and we were very tired. Suddenly, a power boat pulled up to us and a river policeman shouted to us to hold on to a rope. A quarter of an hour later, three weary and bedraggled boys were in the Brighton police station.

That was the end of our last attempt to run away from Perkins. Shortly, a teacher arrived in a car and took us back to school. We expected that we would be in big trouble, but the principal was so relieved to learn that we were safe and sound that we were not even punished.

I kept thinking of what the wandering minstrel had told us about how his music had allowed him to travel anywhere he wanted to go, even in Europe. I had not given much thought before to what I wanted to do in my life, but now I was convinced that nothing could be more exciting than to be a wandering minstrel.

Up to this time, I had been rather bored by music, even though the Perkins School chorus was one of the best in the world. Now I resolved to be the best singer in the chorus and to learn to play the piano.

To get into the chorus, I first had to have a voice test in the music room, where a teacher struck a note on the piano.

"Can you sing that?" he asked.

"Sure," I replied, and sang the note.

"Now, try this one," said the teacher, and played a higher note. I took a deep breath and sang like a thrush.

We continued like this for about five minutes. Then

The Dream of Tomorrow

the teacher spun around on the piano stool and said, "Tommy, you have a very fine voice indeed, and you have perfect pitch."

I was elated. I was one step nearer to being a wandering minstrel.

But there were a great many steps yet to travel. At the same time I joined the chorus, I started to take piano lessons. In my first lesson the piano teacher, Mr. Hank Santos, taught me to feel where the piano keys were. It may have been my inability to see them that eventually became an advantage because I quickly learned to play by my sense of touch.

Mr. Santos was black and a friend of the great black leader Dr. Martin Luther King, Jr. When I was bored and tired of practicing scales on the piano, Mr. Santos was always ready to stop a lesson and talk about the struggle of the black people for civil rights. Because I am truly color blind, I found myself understanding the dreams of the black people.

One evening Mr. Santos took me to his home and introduced his dinner guest, Dr. King. "This is one of my students at the Perkins School for the Blind," said Mr. Santos.

The black leader took my hand in a firm grip and said, "We are all blind in many ways, Tommy. Perhaps you are going to help us lift the blindfolds from our eyes."

At the time I did not quite appreciate what Dr. King meant. But since that meeting, I have often thought of the black leader's words to me.

Not long after my meeting with Dr. King, the Perkins School chorus was invited to sing at the White House by President Lyndon B. Johnson. History began to come alive for me when the Perkins' bus was driven through the gates on Pennsylvania Avenue and we went into the house where so many great men, as well as a few infamous ones, have lived. As we were led into the East Room, I half expected to bump into Abraham Lincoln or Franklin D. Roosevelt.

After the concert was over, the President was introduced to each one of us. Mr. Paul Baugus, the music director, said, "This is Tommy Sullivan, Mr. President."

"How do you do, Mr. President," I greeted as he shook my hand.

"What are you going to be when you grow up, Tommy?" Mr. Johnson asked me.

"I'm not sure, sir," I replied. "I'd like to do something important." I thought he might laugh if I told him I planned to be a wandering minstrel.

"There is something special for every one of you to do," said the President. "How long have you been blind?"

"Since I was born, Mr. President."

"Remember," said Mr. Johnson, "that no experience is a bad experience unless you gain nothing from it."

Then the President moved down the line to the next boy.

I'm sure that President Johnson never thought about me again; but I often thought of what he said to me, especially when I had setbacks and disappointments.

The Dream of Tomorrow

I had to understand that because I was blind, there were many things I would never be able to do. For example, I could never be a baseball umpire or a catcher in the outfield. But every day I was learning that there were more and more things that I *could* do as well or better than boys who had physical vision. Because I was handicapped, I was determined to strive even harder at the sports, the skills, and the work that I could do. Like Martin Luther King, I had a dream—one dream after another.

In my dreams, I rode horseback, sailed boats, played golf, waterskied, traveled to far-away places. In my dreams, my music was heard by millions of people.

Now it was up to me to make my dreams come true.

A Giant Step

Like every high school kid, I longed for the day when I would graduate. I just wanted to get on with life. I wanted to be an adult as quickly as possible and to have the freedom to make my own decisions.

At seventeen, I felt more like an adult than a kid. I felt sure I could make my own way in the world. Of course, I knew there were many things I could not do and would never be able to do. I couldn't be a surgeon, for example, or an airplane pilot, or a cop. There would be an awful lot of accidents if I ever tried to direct traffic!

Yet there were so many things I felt that I could do, and I was eager to get on with it. Not so long ago it was thought that blind people should be given "sheltered employment," and most blind people worked at things like basket weaving or piano tuning, or else they became telephone operators.

But now blind people hold a great variety of jobs. There are many who are successful lawyers, stockbrokers, teachers, research scientists, secretaries, business men and women, psychologists, and radio announcers.

A Giant Step

I still wasn't sure what I wanted to do with my life, but I had some strong ideas. I liked the idea of being a school counselor or a psychologist. I discovered that even though I was a student, many people wanted to talk to me about their problems.

For instance, I might get on a bus and the person sitting next to me, realizing that I was blind, would tell me his problems. Complete strangers, two or three times my age, would talk to me about difficult decisions they had to make. Sometimes they would talk about the most intimate things in their lives, perhaps more freely because they felt I would not recognize them again.

I began to understand that everyone needs someone to talk to—someone who cares and who is willing to listen, or even someone who doesn't care but is willing to listen. I listened a lot. Occasionally, I gave advice. I wasn't sure it was always the best advice, and it took me a while to discover that advice was not what they wanted—only that they be listened to. (That's what is known as nondirective counseling, as I was to discover later.) Listening led me to the notion that it might be a good idea to study what makes people do the things they do and how to overcome behavioral problems.

I remember once on a winter's day sitting next to a young woman who was terribly depressed. She started talking as though she could not contain her problems another moment. She told me that her husband had gone to jail, that she had a small child, and that she had lost her job.

"Life just isn't worth living," she said. "I think I'm

going back home right now and take some sleeping pills. Maybe that will solve all my problems."

I was very concerned because suddenly I felt that her life might depend on what I said to her. I changed the subject, strangely prompted by some inner impulse.

"What's the weather like?" I asked.

"Horrible! It's snowing," said the woman.

"Have you ever heard a snowflake fall?" I asked.

"You've got to be kidding," she replied.

"No, I'm serious," I insisted. "We'll get off at the next bus stop and you can find out. I want you to listen to snowflakes. Only blind people seem to bother to listen to snowflakes fall."

When we were outside, she led me to a bench. As the sound of the traffic receded in the distance, I asked her to listen. Sure enough, when she listened—really listened—she could hear the snowflakes falling. She laughed for the first time, and her desperation seemed to dissipate with the laughter.

I had stepped on a pinecone as we walked to the bench. I felt now until my hands came in contact with another, and I handed it to the woman. "Have you ever really felt a pinecone?" I asked her. "All those little depressions and points are quite different."

"Like people," she replied, as her fingers traveled over the cone, really feeling one for the first time.

"Yes," I agreed. "We've all got different talents and we've all got different lives to live."

She paused and then said, "That's a rather mature statement for a young fellow like you."

We talked some more of how exciting it might be if all of us learned to use all our senses and all our talents.

"This morning you have discovered that even snow makes its own sound," I said. "The next time you go to the sea, try listening to the waves. Some people just hear a roar and a splash. When I listen to a wave, I hear a trillion drops of water all playing their own tune."

"You mean that?" asked the woman.

"Sure," I replied, "You see, I have had to learn about things in a different way from you. Understanding may come more slowly, but perhaps it penetrates more deeply. I'm sure that everyone would discover that life would be so much more fascinating if they only learned to use all their senses."

The woman was quiet for a moment and then she laughed and said, "I think I hear a bus coming."

We ran back to the bus stop, and she said, "You needn't worry about me. I'm going to be okay. I just needed someone to talk to. Thank you for listening."

"Thank you for talking," I said.

I never met this woman again, but I had a feeling that she was going to start experiencing life in a fresh and more exciting way. Anyway, that incident was one of many that helped me to decide to go to college to study psychology.

I received scholarships from Harvard and from Yale, but a friend persuaded me to go to a small college first. Going to Providence College in Rhode Island was a much bigger change than I had expected. The Perkins campus was designed for blind people, but at Providence

College I soon discovered how difficult it was to find my way around. I had to walk all the way across the large campus from one classroom to another, and I often lost my way. I had no Braille books; and instead of taking notes the way most students do, I had to record the lectures on a tape recorder. The cassette recorder had not yet been invented, and my machine was heavy and clumsy. I had to thread the tape onto spools. Sometimes I found that I had threaded the tape incorrectly, but only after I discovered yards of tape tangled at my feet.

I was the first blind student to attend Providence College. I didn't know anybody. When I went to the cafeteria, I bumped into tables and spilled food and coffee. The other students, at first not realizing that I could not see, would get mad at me. I was always bumping into half-open doors.

I was miserable and lonely. At Perkins I had won a U.S. national wrestling title. I had graduated with straight A's. I thought of myself as a first-rate guy. But at Providence I was at the bottom of the totem pole, as they say; and I realized how difficult it was going to be for me to make my way in the sighted world. I was beginning to feel completely alone.

I had just about decided to return to the protection of a blind institution when I met a student who helped to change my thinking. One day I was taking a shower and I dropped the soap. I was feeling around the slippery tiles for it when, from the next shower, a very deep voice asked, "What's the matter with you? Are you blind or something?"

A Giant Step

"Yes," I said.

The deep voice then told me that if I felt six inches off my left foot, I would find the soap.

When I had finished my shower, the student led me back to my room. I could tell from his bony elbow that he had to be very thin, and from where his voice was coming that he had to be at least six feet six inches tall.

"I'm Tom Sly," he grunted. "Are you going to join the freshman against the sophomores?"

"What's that?" I asked.

Tom explained that this was the day when the freshmen at the college "declared war" on the sophomores. The idea was for the men in the freshmen dorms to create as much mess as possible in the sophomore dorms—and vice versa. The only rule was that violence was prohibited.

"Somehow we've got to get inside the sophomore dorm," explained Tom, "but they are guarding the doors like a dictator's palace. I think you could be useful."

"How?" I asked.

"You could pretend to be lost," said Tom.

We spent the next hour, before the "war" was declared, filling balloons with water. Then I was led to a sophomore dorm. I was carrying my white cane and no sophomore stopped me when I walked through the front entrance. I found my way to the bathroom at the back of the building and opened a window. Fifty freshmen, led by Tom Sly, climbed into the enemy territory. Before the sophomores discovered our invasion, the freshmen class had placed water-filled balloons inside all the mattresses of the sophomore dorm. The sophomores didn't get much sleep that night!

What a difference friendship can make! Tom Sly suddenly made the difference between my wanting to leave school and my wanting to stay; he became my closest friend. There was never a shortage of things to talk about or things to do.

Providence College was an all-male school—no girls allowed! One evening, my friends and I thought we should have a dormitory party and invite our girl friends. The problem was how to smuggle them onto the campus and into the dorm without their being seen. The captain of the hockey team, Phil Souza, suggested that we smuggle them in in hockey bags. I helped a girl named Marie into a hockey bag, zipped it shut, and slung it over my shoulder. I entered the dorm elevator; but by the unhappiest chance, the Dean of Discipline, the Rev. Raymond St. George, entered the elevator then.

"Ah! Tom," said the Dean, "I didn't know you played hockey! It must be very hard for you to follow the puck."

I stammered, "Well, I . . . you see . . . it is difficult."

"I'd really like to see how you play," said the Dean. "Perhaps I'll come and watch you tomorrow night."

I don't know how Marie, inside the hockey bag, managed to keep from laughing. I told the Dean that he would be welcome to come and see me on the ice.

I had never put on ice skates before in my life. Anyone who has ever skated knows how hard and painful it is to learn even to keep your balance. Next day, Phil Souza gave me five hours of coaching, but I was still falling about every third step. I was covered with bruises and my ankles and calves were aching by the time the Dean of Discipline arrived. I spent about three minutes wobbling about on the ice and, of course, never coming anywhere near the puck.

Eventually the Dean stood up and said with a quiver in his voice, "Tom, I think you are very courageous to try this sport, but you ought to try an easier game."

"Yes, sir," I replied, and then realized that this was my chance to suggest that Providence College introduce a wrestling program. The Dean agreed at once to help. I became the Providence wrestling coach and for the first time found myself teaching sighted people. Our wrestling program became so popular that Providence beat Brown University and Boston College in the next season. That was the year in which I won an AAU wrestling title.

Although I never played ice hockey again, I was always ready to try almost any sport in which sight was not essential.

I learned to ride horses, both English and Western style, and loved it because it gave me a new sense of freedom. It was a tremendous thrill to gallop over open country. I even started jumping low hurdles with another rider at my side. The other rider would tell me how many paces we were to the jump. Then I could feel my horse gather for the leap. At first I took a good many falls, but eventually I managed to keep in the saddle most of the time.

Another big thrill for me was learning to water-ski. Like everyone else who starts this sport, I spent a lot of time thrashing around in the water; but gradually I learned to keep my balance. I listened to the roar of the speedboat, which told me when to change direction. Once I had gained confidence on two skis I started slalom skiing—that is, using a single ski with two footholds. Slalom skiing is much harder to master; but with my improving sense of balance, I managed quite well.

Learning to play golf was another challenge I accepted—a frustrating but fascinating experience. At first I often missed the ball altogether. One of the secrets of playing good golf is "to keep your eye on the ball." Well, I couldn't very well do that, so I had to work on a "grooved" swing—that is, making certain that the arc formed by the end of the club was always the same.

I had to have a good caddy to place my club alongside the ball. When I was putting, I paced out the distance between my ball and the flag. The caddy had to tell me whether the green was fast or slow, and whether I was hitting uphill or downhill. What a thrilling day it was for me when I first went around an 18-hole course with a score under a hundred. I even had a birdie!

All the time I was trying new things, I was gaining confidence in myself. I was realizing, too, that I could do many things that had at first seemed beyond my capability.

One day, Tom Sly and I were talking to a man who had been a paratrooper in the Vietnam War. The paratrooper, Jack Schula, suddenly said to me, "Tom, that's something you could do!"

A Giant Step

"What?" I asked.
"Skydive," said Jack.
"Me!" I laughed.

But the more Jack talked about the thrill of skydiving, the more I wanted to try this sport.

Jack belonged to a skydiving club at Springfield, Massachusetts, and he drove Tom Sly and me out there one weekend. I soon discovered that you don't just strap on a parachute and jump out of an airplane. There is a lot of preliminary training. First of all, you have to learn to jump off a truck traveling over open ground at twenty miles an hour. There is a special way to jump so that you don't break a leg, or your neck. My wrestling experience helped on that score. I could jump without getting hurt.

After the preliminary training, I was ready to take my first jump from an airplane. Tom Sly had been learning to parachute with me. One problem we had to overcome was how I would know when I was about to hit the ground so that I could roll over in the proper way. Jack and Tom conceived a way. They fixed up a small transceiver in a football helmet. This tiny radio had its bands preset. I could receive instructions from both the pilot of the plane and the ground control. I would be told exactly when to pull the ring on my chute and how far I was from the ground at all times.

I was particularly exhilarated by the fact that I had never heard of a blind person who had skydived. I suppose it is typical that every individual wants to be unique in some respect.

"Okay," said Jack. "Ready to go up?"

"Sure," I replied, and I hoped that Jack would not notice my anxiety or hear my heart thumping.

I climbed into the Piper Cub. Jack repeated the drill instructions.

He said, "Tom, we're going to make two runs across the landing area at thirty-five hundred feet. I want you to jump first, and I will jump just after you. If anything should go wrong with the radio in your helmet, you will be able to hear me shouting at you. When you jump out of the plane, remember to push off with your feet as hard as you can, otherwise you might get hit by the tail of the plane."

I was trying to listen to Jack, but I was really thinking how far it was down there to the ground. There is still time, I thought, to tell Jack that I didn't think my skydiving was such a great idea. I guess I was even more reluctant to let him know I was scared. I was too chicken to chicken out!

"What happens if the parachute fails to open?" I asked.

"If you feel the harness on the left side of your chest," said Jack, "you will find a second ring above the lower ring. Remember, it is the bottom ring that you must pull first. Count five seconds and then pull. If, within a second or two, you don't feel a tug on your shoulders, you must pull the other ring. That second ring will release the spare chute."

I didn't dare ask Jack what would happen if the spare chute failed to open! But then, of course, I also

A Giant Step

knew that skydiving accidents are very rare.

Suddenly, above the roar of the plane, the pilot said, "Going to make the final run across the safe landing area. I will almost stall the plane, so we'll be traveling very slowly. I'll count three, then you jump."

"And I'll be right behind you," said Jack reassuringly.

People have often said to me that it must be easier for me to skydive because I can't see how far I am going to fall. But I don't think this is true. For me, it was like a sighted person jumping on a pitch dark night. Not many skydivers would like to do that.

Then the pilot spoke firmly, "Okay, Tom, one ... two ... three."

I stood up and threw myself head forward out into space. The feeling in the pit of my stomach was like the one you have in a fast-decending elevator—only more so. I remembered to count to five, and then I pulled the lower ring on my harness. Almost immediately I felt a sharp tug on my shoulders as the chute blossomed above me and the harness took up the strain. I was now falling at a rate between twenty and thirty miles an hour. The noise in my ears was like the sound you hear inside a car when a window is open. I was very excited. I began to shout and sing. Then I heard Jack shouting, "Isn't it great?"

Jack had delayed opening his own chute so that we would not get tangled up. I knew Jack would hit the ground ahead of me.

I felt like a bird, with my body in a sitting position,

swinging in slow, lazy arcs and the wind whistling in my ears. This had to be the greatest sensation in the world, I thought.

All too quickly, the transceiver in my helmet crackled, "Okay, Tom, you have three hundred feet to go before hitting the ground."

Now I had to remember all the things I had learned to do so as not to injure myself when I landed. I knew I would be hitting the ground at the same speed as if I had jumped off a wall fourteen feet high. That kind of jump can give you quite a jolt—or even break a leg—unless your body is prepared to take up the shock.

My legs had to be straight down. As I couldn't see the ground, I had to feel my legs with my hands. When I was sure that my legs were straight under the chute, I flexed my knees. If my knees were bent too much I would simply collapse and perhaps seriously injure my spine. I had to put my chin on my chest so that I would roll forward and not backward. Then I had to fold my arms across my chest so that I wouldn't fall on an arm and break it.

The radio in my helmet crackled again; it was ground control. "Tom, you have two hundred feet to go before hitting ... one hundred fifty ... seventy ... Get ready to hit."

Then a thump and a roll and I was back on my world again ... all in one piece.

For a moment or two I just lay on the ground and roared with laughter. I guess I was really tremendously relieved that I was still alive, but I was also enormously

A Giant Step

excited. In fact, that day I made two more jumps. On the third jump the pilot took me up to 6,500 feet, so I had much more time to swing in those lovely, lazy arcs, all the while singing for joy. I had added another dimension to my life.

Falling in Love

After two wonderful years at Providence, I went on to Harvard to complete my degree in psychology. I was especially interested in working with children who had learning difficulties. As an assistant to a famous doctor, I learned that many young children who seem to be backward are not really backward at all. At least, they can achieve more than has been suspected. Some may even catch up and overtake the progress of other children.

There was one little girl who was making no progress at all at school, and her parents and teachers thought she was just stupid. The doctor and I discovered that she was partially deaf. Her deafness was the cause of her slow progress. It was not that she did not understand what her teachers and parents were saying; she didn't *hear* what they were saying. As soon as this child was fitted with a hearing aid, she caught on quickly and soon moved to the head of the class.

There are so many children with physical disabilities that retard their mental development simply because adults do not recognize the problem. Being blind helped

Falling in Love

me to understand, and I was happy to be able to help some of the children we worked with lead normal lives.

Although I was fascinated by the idea of making psychology my career, I was even more attracted by another career possibility. I had grown to love music passionately. I started composing my own songs; and just for fun, I began to play and sing in the lounge of Lowell House at Harvard. The students encouraged my performances, and I enjoyed their applause. I began to write more and more songs.

The melody of a new tune or the words of a song often came to me in the still of the night. I kept a tape recorder beside my bed and I dictated the words or hummed the tune, as the case might be, into the recorder. The next morning I would ask a friend to transcribe the tune into written form.

When the summer vacation came around, my dad, who owned several clubs, helped me get an audition at a new club called Deacon's Perch, on the Cape Cod coast. The audition went well. I was taken on as an entertainer. It was exciting to earn money by doing something I so thoroughly enjoyed, and I was one step closer to that old dream of becoming a wandering minstrel.

Most of the people who came to the club were from the yachts and cruisers anchored off the coast. During the day, I was always invited to go sailing or water-skiing. Then, at night, I would go back to the club to play and sing. During intermissions I talked to the customers. I met a lot of interesting people that way.

One evening when I took a break from my playing

and weaved my way among the tables, a cheerful voice said, "Congratulations! We loved your singing."

"Thanks a lot," I replied.

The girl said, "Wouldn't you like to sit with us for a moment? My name is Connie, and my friend's name is Patty. We're sophomores at the University of Arizona and we have summer jobs as waitresses at the Wheelhouse."

The Wheelhouse was a well-known restaurant not far from Deacon's Perch.

I joined them and asked, "Why don't we have supper together after the club closes?"

Connie said, "I'm afraid we can't. We are on the early shift at the restaurant and we'll have to get some sleep. Somebody told us that the music here was great. That's why we're here."

The other girl put out her hand and spoke for the first time. She asked, rather shyly, "Are you really blind?"

I laughed and replied, "How else do you think I could tell that you are a blonde, that you're five feet five inches tall, and that you weigh one hundred fifteen pounds?"

"One hundred seventeen pounds," laughed Patty.

I didn't tell Patty that almost as soon as a person shakes my hand I can guess his or her weight, and fairly accurately. Obviously, if a hand is pudgy and the body is short, the person is sure to be plump, at least. I knew that Patty was about average height because as soon as she spoke, I knew how high her mouth was above the table. From her handshake I knew she was neither fat nor thin. And I am usually right in guessing the color of a per-

Falling in Love

son's hair. Blonds and brunettes seem to have different tonal qualities in their voices. Of course, Connie and Patty were really puzzled and weren't quite sure that I was totally blind.

It was fun to keep them guessing for a while. Before I returned to the stage, the two girls invited me to join them for a beach picnic the following day.

"We'll bring the chicken," said Connie, "and we'll pick you up in the Beast."

"What's the Beast?" I asked. "Is it a horse, elephant, or a camel?"

"It's our car," explained Connie. "We bought it for eighty dollars. It won't go in reverse and the starter doesn't work."

Next day at about noon I heard a car horn outside the room I had rented. I went outside to investigate and found Patty sitting in their very old car.

"Hi," called Patty. "The engine's stopped, so do you mind pushing to get the Beast started?"

"Where's Connie?" I asked, with a slight tinge of disappointment in my voice. I hoped it wasn't apparent.

"Afraid she couldn't come," said Patty. "Her parents arrived unexpectedly. Do you mind having a picnic with me?"

I got behind the Beast and started to push. Eventually the motor fired. Breathless and sweating, I jumped in beside Patty.

"Would you like me to drive?" I asked.

Patty laughed, and her laughter was musical and full of fun, full of life. I was suddenly glad that Connie had not been able to come.

We found a quiet place on the beach and spread a blanket on the sand. Patty dropped the chicken in the sand, and when I bit into a drumstick, I chipped a tooth. "I hope you're going to pay my dentist's bill," I said, pretending to be cross.

After we had finished lunch, Patty pulled me to my feet and said she wanted to walk. The sun was warm and the only sounds were from the seagulls and the small waves lapping at the shoreline. It suddenly seemed to me that we were the only people in the world.

We walked and we talked. I spoke about my own childhood and how my parents and relatives had always wanted to protect me—how they seemed determined to keep me from leading a normal life.

"But even as a boy I wanted to do all the things that other boys did—climb trees, toboggan in winter, surf and sail in the summer. I was always unhappy about not being able to catch a ball, and I have often asked myself, 'Why was I blind? Why me?' I still don't know the answer."

Patty was silent for a while; then she said unexpectedly, "Perhaps there is a reason. There is a reason for almost everything."

"What do you mean?" I asked.

"I'm not quite sure," said Patty. "But you seem to have done so many things that people with sight have never attempted to do. Maybe you can inspire many people who think they have problems." She squeezed my hand and laughed happily. "I think you are wonderful!

Falling in Love

Certainly, you inspire me. When I heard you singing last night, I felt sure that I was listening to someone who could become a famous artist."

Patty talked quietly and with such positive conviction that I felt really good. I had never met anyone like her before. She talked of God, and she said she believed that God had a plan for everyone, including me. She said, "I guess you've got to have faith."

"Faith is a pretty hard thing to have when you are blind," I replied.

"Faith is rather like love—you either have it or you haven't," said Patty. Then she went on to tell me of her own childhood and how sickly she had been, even critically ill when she was a small child. The doctor told her parents that if they wanted her to grow up, they would have to move from the cold winters of Michigan to the dry Arizona desert.

"My dad had a successful business, which he had built up himself," said Patty. "But Dad put my life before security and everything else. He sold his business and moved to Tucson, Arizona, where he had to start all over again. We had very little money, but that didn't worry Dad because my health improved and I became strong again. Then Dad's new business began to grow. I guess you could call that faith."

We walked and talked for such a long time that we had not realized how late it was. Patty suddenly said, "I wish you could see the beautiful sunset. It doesn't mean much to you if I talk about red and orange clouds, does it? How do you see a sunset?"

I thought about the question for a moment and then said, "For me, a sunset is like taking a thousand pieces of glass of different shapes and letting them fall to form their own patterns. A sunset is like closing the day with happiness."

"That's beautiful!" exclaimed Patty.

"Well, one of the advantages of being blind," I said, "is that I don't see ugly things in the same way that you do. I don't see factories spewing their pollution into the air or junkyards or litter in the streets and parks. As a matter of fact, I've never seen an ugly person. When a sighted person says, 'Oh, he's ugly' or 'She's pretty,' I realize that I can't make a visual interpretation that way. I can't make quick judgments of people. I have to concentrate more on everyone I meet. I have to interpret them with my senses of touch and smell and sound. I form my opinions of people more slowly, I guess."

Patty said, "But there must be some things you don't like."

"Oh sure," I replied, "I hate the smell of skunks, and I hate the sound of an ambulance. An ambulance siren seems to scream of pain and fear. And I have met many people whom I don't get along with—but not because of the way they look. Old people with wrinkles or deformed people can be very beautiful people to me. I don't see their leathery skins and twisted limbs. I see inside them. An old voice often means experience and wisdom and tolerance. A rough hand tells me someone has worked hard."

"Can you tell a lot from a handshake?" asked Patty.

Falling in Love

"Much more than you can guess," I said. "Haven't you ever noticed that a person who just gives you a fingertip handshake is not very interested in you? But the handshake of a friend—ah! That's quite different. When most people shake hands, they look at the expression on a person's face. But the face can be a mask. People don't realize how much they say when they shake hands."

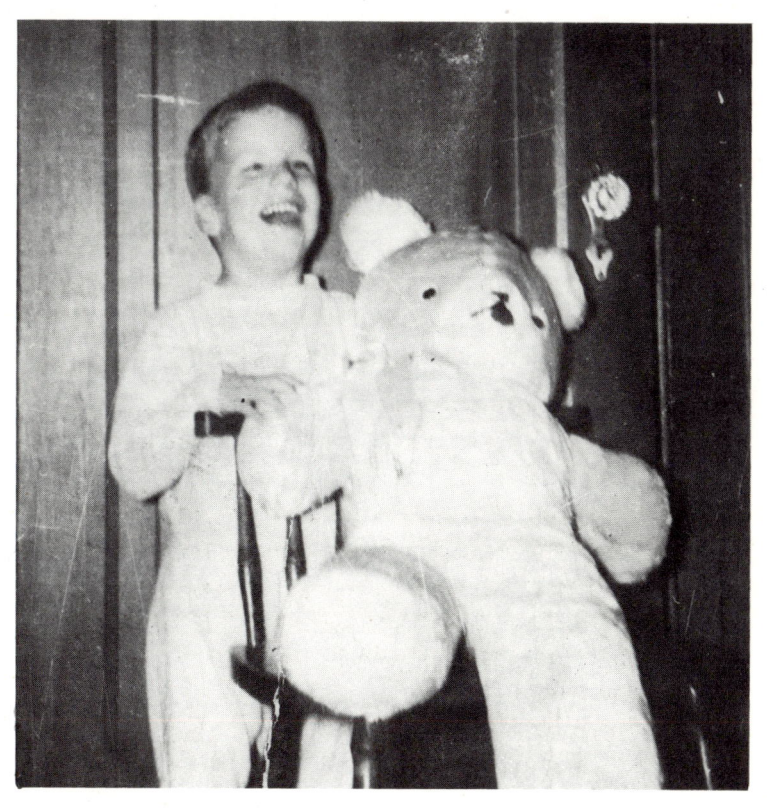

A large, fuzzy Teddy bear was a great companion for Tommy, who loved the feel of its fur.

"How else do you judge a person when you first meet?" asked Patty.

"You can tell a great deal from the way a person walks," I said. "If I hear heavy slow footsteps, I know that the walker is older or tired or fed up. If the footsteps are brisk and firm, then I know that the walker knows where he is going or is excited about something."

"What about my footsteps?" asked Patty.

"You don't walk; you dance!" I replied. "That means you must be very happy."

"I don't think I've ever been happier," she laughed.

"Nor I," I said and gave her a hug.

We stopped walking and sat for a while on some rocks. Then we felt around in the pools of water for shells and sea urchins. I told Patty how much I loved to feel living things like leaves and flowers, the bark of trees, the fur of a dog, the flank of a horse.

"And the silk of your hair," I said. "It's the silkiest hair I have ever touched."

We were silent for a while and the air was charged with feeling. Both of us knew what was happening—we were falling in love. It was the strangest feeling. There was an ache in my heart and the feeling in my stomach was like the one I had the first time I skydived.

Then Patty broke the silence. She said, "I only wish we had met earlier. Then we could have had the whole summer ahead of us. But I have to fly back to Arizona tomorrow."

My heart sank. "I wonder if we'll ever meet again," I said sadly.

Falling in Love

Patty replied quickly, "You could try having faith. I believe that if we are meant to meet again, we will meet again. Let's not think about tomorrow. The sun has not quite gone down. Let's think about today."

"What about a swim?" I suggested

"Lovely," she exclaimed. "And there is no one else on the beach. We can pretend we are on our own tropical island. See if you can catch me."

Patty started to run down the beach. I had to listen for her footsteps and then I chased her. When I caught her, I carried her into the sea. She was a strong swimmer, and we swam together far out. Patty swam away from me and then shouted, "Now, see if you can catch me."

I listened, but I couldn't hear her. I guessed she had ducked under the surface. I put my head below the surface and then I could distinctly hear bubbles. I swam toward the bubbles and Patty was surprised when I grabbed her ankle.

"But how did you know?" she asked.

"Because I used my ears for eyes," I laughed.

That night when Patty arrived at the club, I sang one of my own songs. It was titled "Every Time I Fall in Love, I Fall in Love with You." I put real feeling into the words that night, and the audience responded with long applause. I guessed that Patty knew I was singing especially for her.

One of the visitors at the club was the talent scout for *The Johnny Carson Show*. When I took a break, this man came over to see me.

He said, "You sang that song as if you're really in

love." Then he invited me to sing it on *The Johnny Carson Show*.

I was waiting for Patty to come for me and take me to her table. I was eager to tell her about the invitation to appear on television with Johnny Carson. I was puzzled that she hadn't yet come. Then one of the waiters, who was a friend of mine, tapped me on the shoulder and said, "A young lady asked me to give you this note."

"Is it written in Braille?" I asked.

"No."

"Then you'd better read it to me," I said.

The waiter read the note, which was written on a paper napkin. The note read, "I'm afraid I would cry if I said good-bye to you. I love you. Have faith that we'll meet again—Patty."

Suddenly, I felt terribly empty and lonely. At first I was bitterly disappointed that Patty had not said 'good-bye' to me. I even began to think that she didn't want to see me again because I was blind. The excitement of being invited to appear on *The Johnny Carson Show* began to fade. What I wanted more than anything else in the world was to be with Patty. I wanted to hear her laughter, which sounded more like music to me than any song. Then, as I sat there, lonely and despondent, I remembered Patty's words, "Have faith that we'll meet again." I felt better. I went back to the piano.

My First TV Appearance

Up to now, I had played and sung to small audiences—to students in the lounge at school and to customers at Deacon's Perch. But singing on *The Johnny Carson Show* would mean that millions of people would hear me. A dream was on the edge of reality. It was like moving from the Little League into Big League baseball. I was very nervous.

When I was standing in the wings, awaiting my turn to go onstage, my throat felt so tight that I didn't think I would be able to sing a note. I was sure that when I opened my mouth, no sound would come out.

Then I remembered Patty, and I thought, "I will sing especially for her. I won't think of the millions of people watching television. I will think only of one person whom I love very much, and I will sing only to her." My throat relaxed.

Just at that moment, a man came to the dressing room and asked, "Are you ready, Mr. Sullivan? You're onstage in three minutes."

Those seemed like the longest three minutes of my

life. I was led to the stage; and I heard Mr. Carson saying to the audience, "I want you to give a big welcome to a young new artist, Tom Sullivan. This is an important night because I believe that Tom is going to be a star."

Mr. Carson did not say anything about my being blind, and I don't believe that anyone in the audience at first realized that I could not see. I don't think they knew until I had sung my song and Mr. Carson came to me and linked his arm through mine. He guided me to a seat beside him. We talked mostly about golf, which Mr. Carson enjoys playing. I accepted his invitation to play with him, but said I wasn't quite ready to take him on at tennis! Everyone laughed.

Mr. Carson has a way of putting people at ease, which is one of the reasons he is such a successful host and entertainer. What I didn't expect was the large number of messages of congratulations I received. I was beginning to realize that I really could step into the "Big League" of the entertainment world. Following that appearance, several of the major record companies invited me to make an album.

The days were very full for me. When I wasn't recording, I was entertaining at clubs or studying psychology. But there was still an emptiness in my life which followed me around. I longed to be with Patty again. We were separated by several thousand miles; and although we talked quite often on the telephone, it was not the same as being together.

Sometimes, when I was very lonely and missing Patty, I would ask Jack Schula to take me skydiving. The

My First TV Appearance

excitement of skydiving helped take my mind off my loneliness. But skydiving took its toll. I often made bumpy landings, and this may have been one of the reasons that I developed glaucoma in my eyes. With sighted people, glaucoma is considered a serious disease because it can lead to blindness. For me, the seriousness was that I suffered severe headaches.

One very cold night, I was working in my dormitory room when my head began to hurt so badly that I thought it was going to explode. I took some aspirin, but they didn't help at all. I had to get medication which was stronger than aspirin from the Harvard infirmary, so I made my way out of the dorm and into the freezing weather outside. The snow muffled all sound. Snow is a blind man's fog.

I thought I was walking across Harvard Square when I suddenly slipped on a sheet of ice. I was dazed and had no idea where I was. The pain in my head throbbed, and I just lay there in the snow. I didn't want to move.

I don't like to think what might have happened if another student had not walked across the square at that time. But someone must have been looking after me for I heard a voice above me saying, "Are you okay? Can I help?"

The student helped me to my feet and, discovering that I was blind, led me to the infirmary. There a doctor gave me a pain-killing shot and I was taken to Massachusetts General Hospital. An ophthalmologist told me that the only way I could get rid of the headaches was to have my eyes surgically removed and replaced with artifical ones.

That may sound like a horrible thing to have happen, but for me it didn't matter. Mine had never been of any use to me. Besides, this way I could choose whatever color eyes I wanted! And even change them when I wished. Actually, I asked for brown eyes because brown was the natural color of my eyes. The doctor promised me that my plastic eyes would look much better than my real ones.

The operation was successful. The headaches disappeared, and I was grateful for that. But no doctor could heal the pain in my heart—the pain caused by my longing to be with Patty.

I had definitely decided that I wanted to marry her, but I was tortured by the thought that it might not be right for the girl I loved to have a blind husband. All the time I felt that I had to prove that I could hold down a good job, or at least earn enough money to support her and give her a nice home.

One day, I had been worrying about my future so much that I asked Jack Schula to take me skydiving. Skydiving always seemed to clear my head and help me forget my worries. When we reached the flying club, the pilot of the plane shook his head.

"The wind is too gusty. It wouldn't be safe for you to jump today," he said.

I protested that Jack and I had traveled a long way and explained that I was an experienced skydiver. The pilot was still not too keen on it, but reluctantly agreed

My First TV Appearance

to take me up.

At about 6,500 feet the little plane was tossing about in the gusty wind. The pilot suddenly said, "Okay, Tom ... one ... two ... three ... jump."

Once again I thrilled to the feeling of complete abandon as I dived into space. I waited for Jack or ground control to tell me when to pull the ring to release the parachute. But the little radio was silent. I suddenly realized that the radio wasn't working. Because we were talking so much about the weather, I had forgotten to check the batteries in the transceiver in my helmet. Momentary panic! My mind raced! Because the wind could blow me far from the safe landing area, I delayed pulling the chute for about forty seconds. I knew, though, what a dangerous situation I was in. It was impossible for me to tell how far above the ground I was. Also Jack had warned me about trees and high-tension wires not far from the landing field.

Without my knowing when to bend my knees to take up the shock of landing, and guessing that the wind was taking me away from the safe landing area, I realized that I might even be killed.

If the radio in my helmet had been working, Jack or ground control could have helped guide me away from danger. By pulling the ropes of the harness in certain ways, a parachutist can alter his course and compensate for drift.

The strangest thing about my predicament was that I wasn't frightened. I thought of Patty; perhaps that was the reason.

Often, in times of great danger, the mind works more efficiently. The most important thing is to avoid panic. Panic seems to paralyze rational action. You often hear of people caught in a burning building doing crazy things like jumping from a third-story window, when, if they had remained calm, they could have saved themselves from serious injury or even death.

Of course, I couldn't do very much as I swung about under my parachute except relax and pray a little. But I was alert for the shock of landing, whenever it happened.

One firm decision I came to as I drifted downward was that if I survived the jump, I would fly to Arizona. I would tell Patty how much I loved her and that more than anything else in the world, I wanted to marry her and take care of her for the rest of our lives.

I had just made a sort of vow to that effect when suddenly I crashed. Pain shot through my right arm and my ribs. There was a sound of ripping cloth and snapping branches. I had landed in a tree!

For a few seconds the cords of the chute wrapped around a branch and I was poised thirty feet above the ground. Then the branch snapped and I fell the rest of the way. It was a hard landing. I knew I had a broken arm, but I was quite conscious. At least I was alive.

When Jack and some friends arrived to help me, they asked my why my fingernails were bleeding. It was only then that I remembered how I had dug my fingers into the frozen ground because I was so glad to be back on earth—and alive!

My broken arm was set and put in a plaster cast. My

My First TV Appearance

broken ribs were strapped and my scratches were cleaned. Within a few days I was hobbling about again, and within a month I was ready to fly to Arizona.

I had wired Patty that I was coming. When I got off the plane, there were many people milling all around me. But above the noise I could distinguish running feet. I would know those footsteps anywhere! A moment later Patty ran into my arms. My white cane and suitcase were knocked out of my hands. I lifted her off her feet and we just spun around in a sort of dance. I guess everyone was looking at us, but that didn't matter. I could feel Patty's cheeks were wet with tears. Then she whispered into my ear, "You see, Tom, what happens when you have faith? I knew we would meet again."

Patty's parents and brothers were worried by the thought of Patty's marrying a blind man. Like so many people, they believed that a blind person was a helpless invalid. Somehow, I had to prove differently.

"Okay," I said to her three brothers, "let's have a game of yard basketball."

"But you can't play basketball," said Joe, Patty's youngest brother.

"Why don't you find out?" I replied.

I asked Patty to stand underneath the basket and to call out every time I got the ball. We played a really hard game, but with Patty shouting, "Shoot, Tom, shoot!" I shot twice as many baskets as Joe.

Then the next day we went riding in the foothills, and after that we played golf. None of them wanted to take me on at wrestling!

Anyway, Patty's brothers soon understood that I wasn't exactly a helpless invalid.

But Mr. Steffan, Patty's father, was another matter. He was harder to convince. I found him alone in his office and went in.

"Good morning, Mr. Steffan," I said cheerfully. "You know that Patty and I want to get married, and I know that you are not at all happy about our plans."

"No, I'm not," replied Mr. Steffan gruffly.

"Why?" I asked.

"You know why," he said. "She is my very dear and only daughter, and I think it is unfair of you to ask her to marry you. Suppose you have children? Perhaps they will be blind like you."

"Oh, no," I protested. "You're quite wrong, sir. My blindness was caused by an accident in the hospital where I was born. It is not an hereditary defect at all. If we should have children, they will be as clear-sighted as Patty."

"All right," said Mr. Steffan. "I'm glad to hear that. But how are you going to support Patty? It's hard enough for a sighted person to make his way in the world."

"I've just been offered a job as an entertainer at a thousand dollars a week," I said, "and a big record company wants me to make an album."

Mr. Steffan was surprised. Then he said, "I suppose that many people like me think of blind people as being helpless and dependent. You sound to me as if you're going to be a millionaire."

My First TV Appearance

"Yes, I think I am," I said confidently. "But you haven't asked me the most important question."

"What's that?" he asked.

"If I love your daughter," I said.

"Well, do you?"

"I love Patty so much that I would give my life for her," I answered.

Mr. Steffan blew his nose very hard. Then he asked, "Have you set the wedding date?"

That night at a happy family dinner we decided on a spring wedding.

I guess most stories would end at this point. The last line usually reads, "And so we lived happily ever after." But after our wonderful wedding I felt that our story was not ending at all. In fact, I felt that it was just beginning. Besides, it couldn't end until you'd met Heidi and Blythe.

Heidi is a German shepherd. She is not just a family pet. She is a seeing-eye dog—my seeing-eye dog. She once saved my life.

Blythe is our little daughter. She is blonde and lovely like her mother. And I once saved her life!

Vision Unlimited

One evening, Patty leaned over and whispered in my ear, "We're going to have a baby." We were naturally very excited, but I knew that if Patty was to give proper care to a baby, she would have much less time for me. For instance, she would not be as free to drive me to recording studios, clubs, and other places where I worked as an artist.

We were not living near Hollywood. I would need to be more independent, so I told Patty that I thought it was time for me to have a seeing-eye dog. We had a friend who bred German shepherds, and we went to his house to see him. The friend took us to his kennels, and as soon as he opened the gate, nine little bundles of fur ran toward us. The puppies were less than a month old. I knelt down on the ground and the puppies licked my hands and face. Then one puppy pushed its way past its brothers and sisters and rested its head on my knee.

I knew at once that this was the puppy I wanted. Turning to our friend, I said, "This one seems to know me already."

"Oh, that's Heidi," said our friend. "Yes, she has been very special since the day she was born."

"In what way?" I asked.

"Well, Heidi just loves people. She seems to prefer people to her mother and to her brothers and sisters. I guessed you'd find Heidi."

"I didn't find her," I replied, "Heidi found me."

Patty and I took Heidi home. Heidi followed me everywhere. She even tried to get into my bed. She seemed to say, "I'm not just an ordinary dog. I was born to be your friend and companion. I was born to be your eyes."

Patty told me that Heidi was gray and brown, that her ears were always pointed and alert, and that she never took her eyes off me.

But seeing-eye dogs need to have special training. They have to learn words of command and to protect their master or mistress against all dangers—especially the danger of traffic. They have to get used to a special U-shaped harness. We knew we would have to send Heidi to a school for seeing-eye dogs.

One of the best schools for training seeing-eye dogs is in North Hollywood. The head of the school, Mr. Erik Renner, had commanded German U-boats in World War II. We went to see him.

"No," said Mr. Renner. "I'm sorry, but I cannot take Heidi into my school. Anyway, I only train dogs that I breed myself."

"But Heidi is special," I protested.

Then Mr. Renner explained how he selected puppies to be trained as seeing-eye dogs. He told me how he knew, even when the puppies were only a few weeks old, whether or not they would make good guide dogs.

"There are some puppies that are aggressive. They are born fighters. These dogs are often trained to be police dogs. Other dogs are just meant to be family pets. We never cuddle the puppies that are to be trained as seeing-eye dogs or police dogs," he explained. "The lives of people—of people like you, Tom, and police officers—may depend on the discipline, training, intelligence, and independence of our dogs."

"But Heidi is very intelligent, and I'm sure she can be trained quite easily," I pleaded.

Mr. Renner put his arm on my shoulder and said sympathetically, "I can see that Heidi is a magnificent dog. I only wish I had had her here when she was a puppy. But there is another reason why you would not want to leave Heidi in my school. You might not get her back. We try to match dogs to people, and she might be better suited to someone else. It wouldn't be wise to give a playful, energetic dog to an older person. An older person would need a quieter, steadier dog."

I was very disappointed, but I knew Mr. Renner was a famous dog trainer and knew what he was doing. He was very enthusiastic about his work and took it extremely seriously.

He went on to explain how he trained his German shepherds. The real training starts when they are about ten months old. One of the first lessons is teaching a dog to stop at a curb. Training schools for dogs have recently

Vision Unlimited

adopted a new method of training or conditioning. In the old days, the dog trainer tugged at the leash when a dog reached a curb. Now the trainers use a special collar, wired in such a way as to give the dog an electric shock whenever it does anything wrong. The trainer uses a small radio transmitter to control the device. When the trainer presses a button on the transmitter, two metal prongs on the dog's collar give a sharp jolt to the dog. The collar is also used to train the dog not to chase cats or other animals.

At Mr. Renner's school they have a Siamese cat that deliberately teases the dogs under training. When a dog growls and starts to chase the cat, the trainer presses the transmitter button. The dog gets an eighty-volt shock and stops at once. In a very short while the dog understands that cats must not be chased.

If a seeing-eye dog was fond of chasing cats, or other dogs, or squirrels, or cars, the blind person might find himself stranded, perhaps in the middle of a busy street.

A seeing-eye dog under training is taught to watch out for all dangers that might be encountered by a blind person. For instance, a dog is taught to avoid obstacles that might hurt its owner. If a dog were to take its master under a low shop awning, the blind person might bruise or cut his head. At the school, the trainers rig up low obstacles made of bamboo, and if the dog goes near the obstacles, the bamboo falls on top of the dog with such a terrible clatter that the dog avoids low obstacles in the future.

Noise training is also important. Mr. Renner said,

"We take a dog to a public school at the time of recess. When the children pour out of the classrooms, the dog must learn to keep calm and to guide his master through the crowd. This training comes in handy when a blind person goes to a football game or to a busy airport."

"What about unexpected noises like a car backfiring?" I asked.

"Very important," agreed Mr. Renner. "We fire guns just over the heads of dogs in training. The first time, the dog is frightened and cowers; but the good dog soon understands that, although she doesn't like the noise, she must take no notice of it. Can you guess, Tom, what the toughest test is?"

"Traffic," I suggested.

"No, it's the noise of jet planes. We take the dogs to the Los Angeles International Airport and we have special permission to go right onto the runway. The dog has to learn not to retreat when the jets scream for takeoff."

"But the dogs must be frightened," I suggested.

"Oh, sure," said Mr. Renner. "But their training to look after their master must be stronger than their greatest instinct—fear. One thing that always frightens a dog to start with is going up and down a fire escape. The dog can see through the iron steps and know how far he has to fall. But it must learn to be unafraid because the day may come when the dog might have to rescue its master or mistress from a blazing building."

Mr. Renner told me that it takes up to eight months and hundreds of dollars to train one guide dog. By the time a dog is ready to be handed over to a blind person, it is probably the most highly trained animal in the world.

"A seeing-eye dog cannot speak, but it can understand about thirty words," said Mr. Renner.

"What words?" I asked.

"The first word it learns is the same as that a baby learns. That word is 'no.' Then we say 'good girl' if she does the right thing."

"Or, 'good boy,'" I laughed.

"In our school we train only females to be guide dogs," replied Mr. Renner. "We have found that females make the best dogs for blind people."

"What happens to the male dogs?" I asked.

"They are trained to be police dogs, or else we give them away."

"So, the girls are better than the boys," I exclaimed.

"For people like you who need eyes," replied Mr. Renner. "But for other tough jobs, like police work, the males can be just as good or better than the females."

Mr. Renner then told me how German shepherds are employed to track down drug smugglers, burglars, and lost children. He recounted many stories of how dogs make great detectives.

I particularly liked the story about a police dog called Zisca, who was taken to a supermarket because two robbers were known to be hiding inside the building. Zisca went straight to the dog-food counter and started barking. The store manager sneered that Zisca was obviously more interested in his stomach than in catching crooks. They took Zisca outside the store and again ordered him to find the crooks. A second time he went straight to the dog-food counter. On the third try, the same thing happened. They decided to give Zisca one more try. Zisca shot into the supermarket and back to the dog-food counter. But this time he began to tear away at the big sacks of dog food. Concealed behind the sacks, Zisca found the two thieves. The police soon put handcuffs on the crooks, and the store manager was so pleased that he gave Zisca a month's supply of the very best dog food.

Then Mr. Renner told me about a seeing-eye dog called Helga that he had given to a blind college student, Herb Smith. One day, a professor at the college noticed that Helga was tugging at the student and it was obvious that the student wanted to go in the opposite direction.

The puzzled professor asked, "Is there something wrong with your dog, Herb? Can I help?"

"Oh, no," replied Herb. "Helga knows that I'm late for my French class, but I was figuring on skipping class today."

I laughed and suggested that perhaps Helga wanted to learn French.

"That's not quite as funny as it may sound," said Mr. Renner. "We train dogs to understand Spanish for blind, Spanish-speaking people. You could train an intelligent dog to understand basic words in any language —even Chinese."

I could have listened to Mr. Renner all day, but I remembered the main purpose of my visit and tried once more. "If only you understood what it's like to be blind, I know you'd accept Heidi at your school."

"Oh, but I do know what it's like," replied Mr. Renner. "To better understand the problems faced by blind people, I once blindfolded myself for six weeks. During that period I never took the blindfold off. The experience was invaluable to me as a trainer. It's exactly because I *do* understand your difficulties and needs so well that we train our German shepherds to be superdogs. When one of my assistants comes to me and reports that he has a dog ready to be given to a blind person, I ask, 'Okay, would you give this dog to your mother or your brother if he or she were blind?' Often the assistant will shake his head and take the dog back for more training."

"But I still don't understand why you won't take Heidi," I protested.

"Because you love Heidi," said Mr. Renner, "and because she loves you. If Heidi were trained here, we might find that she was not the best dog for you. If you handed Heidi over to me now, you might never see her again."

"I couldn't bear that," I replied, "nor could Patty."

"That's what I thought," said Mr. Renner. "But I've got an idea. One of America's most successful dog trainers has just retired. He now breeds German shepherds in Tucson, Arizona. He just might agree to train Heidi. I'll give you his name and address."

Two days later I flew with Heidi to Tucson to the home of Mr. John Webb, who has spent a lifetime training seeing-eye dogs. It was Mr. Webb who opened the first guide-dog school in Mexico.

I explained to Mr. Webb what my problem was and how the Guiding Eye School in Hollywood had refused to train Heidi unless I took the risk of giving her up to another blind person.

Mr. Webb listened to me and then said firmly, "I don't train dogs anymore. I'm retired. I want time to go fishing. A dog trainer works seven days a week, and I think I've earned my retirement."

Mr. Webb saw my disappointment, but I knew he was watching Heidi closely. Suddenly, he said, "You have a very handsome dog. She looks intelligent. I'll tell you what I'll do. You leave Heidi with me for two months. If after that time I think she'll make a good guide dog, I might agree to train her. I don't want you to see Heidi again until I telephone you."

Heidi seemed to understand our conversation. She came to me and rested her head on my knees. Then she padded across the room and sat down by Mr. Webb.

I missed Heidi terribly when I flew back to Los Angeles. Every day I wanted to phone Mr. Webb to find out how she was getting along, but I didn't dare. Then, two months later, Patty answered the telephone and called breathlessly, "Tom, Mr. Webb is on the phone!"

My heart was pounding when I picked up the phone. "Well?" I asked. "Is it good news?"

Mr. Webb paused. Then he said, "You must have the most intelligent German shepherd I have ever handled. And I've handled hundreds of dogs."

So that was that! Heidi had passed her first exam.

Vision Unlimited

Then, for the next three months, I thought of Heidi undergoing all that hard training, which Mr. Renner had spoken about. I knew that she would have to learn at least thirty words, such as *forward, left, right, bus stop, telephone, elevator, wait, outside, inside, car.*

At last the day came when Mr. Webb telephoned again. He said simply, "Tom, come and pick up your seeing-eye dog. Perhaps you've forgotten her name. She's called Heidi."

I will never forget the moment when Heidi and I met again. I heard the running of padded feet. Then a warm furry body was pressed against my legs. Heidi was trembling from excitement. She seemed to be trying to tell me how proud she was that she'd graduated, and she now understood why we'd been separated for so long.

Mr. Webb said, "Look after her because she is going to look after you. Heidi is no longer just a friendly German shepherd. She is your eyes."

I spent a month with Mr. Webb, who taught me all the things that he had taught Heidi. I learned the words that Heidi would understand. Mr. Webb taught me how to strap on and use the special harness that guide dogs wear when they are working. He demonstrated how Heidi, when she was in harness, should always walk about half a pace in front of me. I began to feel that Heidi was part of me. I felt safe with her, even when crossing a busy street.

By the time our daughter, Blythe, was born, Heidi was taking me almost everywhere, so that Patty could spend much more time with our baby. I often flew from

Today, Tom is happy and looking forward to many more exciting adventures in his life.

Los Angeles to New York for concerts and recordings, and I always took Heidi with me. When I arrived at the airport in a cab, Heidi knew exactly where to take me—to the counter to buy my ticket, onto the plane, through the swinging doors of a hotel, and even to my room. When I gave a concert, Heidi took me to the piano on the stage and sat beside me. She thumped her tail when the audience applauded.

Heidi loves to play with a ball, but she soon discovered it was no good dropping the ball at my feet, where I usually couldn't find it. On her own, she started tossing the ball with her mouth right at my stomach or into my lap.

When I went swimming or water-skiing, Heidi never took her eyes off me. She sat on the beach and barked a warning if she felt I was swimming too far out of my depth. Once, when I was waterskiing, I hit a log and fell with a big splash. The pilot of the speedboat did not at first realize I was floundering in the water. Suddenly, I felt a tug at my life preserver. Heidi had come to my rescue. She began to pull me toward the edge of the lake.

We laughed about this incident because I was not really in danger of drowning. But Heidi wasn't taking any chances.

One day Heidi really did save my life. I had gone for a walk and was returning home when a car screamed around the corner at the end of our street. Heidi had started to guide me across the road to my house. She saw the danger. The car was traveling too fast to avoid running me down. Heidi sprang at my chest and hurled me backward to the sidewalk.

I heard a sickening thud. Heidi had been hit. The driver of the car didn't stop. Heidi was lying beside me, whimpering. When I felt out with my hands to pat her and tell her how grateful I was for her saving me from injury or death, I felt her fur wet with blood.

Patty had heard the screech of car tires. She came

running across the street and put her arms around me.

"I'm okay," I said. "I wasn't hit. But what's happening to Heidi?"

Patty turned to Heidi and saw the horrible gaping wound where the fender of the car had ripped her side. Heidi was shivering and whimpering, but she had enough strength to lick my face when I bent over her. It was as if she were saying, "I did my duty. I saved you, master."

"Good girl," I assured her. "You're a very good girl."

Patty and I carried the limp form of Heidi to our car and we drove at once to the nearest animal hospital. The veterinary surgeon was grave. "We'll X-ray her at once and find out how badly she's hurt," he said.

Patty and I waited on a bench for the doctor to return. It seemed like hours, but I guess it was only about twenty minutes before the doctor walked briskly down the corridor. He said, "Your dog is going to be all right. She is badly bruised, and I had to put in twenty stitches to close up the wound, but there are no broken bones. She will recover."

Poor Heidi limped for a month. Then one morning I felt a ball land in my lap. Heidi was ready to resume her duties as a seeing-eye dog.

But the accident brought us even closer. How do you describe a friend who has saved your life at the risk of her own?

Reaching for Life

Our daughter, Blythe, was born with blond hair and clear blue eyes—eyes that would add new vistas to my world. It was a joy to watch her grow—to hear her first words and the sound of her first uncertain footsteps.

Even as a three-year-old, Blythe loved the water and was fearless in it. And, of course, I wanted her to learn and experience as much of life as possible. I cherished every moment with her.

One lovely summer morning, Blythe danced into our breakfast room and said, "Daddy, let's go swimming."

"Sure, we'll go," I replied. "We can have the whole morning to play because Mommy's going to the store, and I'm going to take a day off from writing music."

We walked to the car with Patty and waved goodbye as she drove off to go shopping. I left Heidi inside the house because she was always nervous and restless whenever she saw Blythe splashing about in the water. I gave Heidi a pat on the head, and said, "It's okay; you look after the house. I'm going to look after Blythe today, and Blythe is going to look after me."

Blythe held my hand and led me down to the pool. But just as we arrived there, the extension telephone at the poolside rang.

"I'll have to answer the phone, Blythe," I said. "You sit on the steps and wait for me."

I couldn't see that Blythe's plastic duck was floating on the water at the deep end of the pool or that Blythe was reaching out to try to catch the duck.

I answered the phone. The call was from one of the big recording studios. They wanted to hear my latest song. Just as I replaced the receiver, I heard a splash. I wasn't worried because I thought Blythe had probably thrown her life preserver into the pool.

I called to her, "Blythe ... Blythe?"

There was no answer. A heavy truck rumbled down the road beyond the garden hedge, and I thought Blythe had not heard me.

"Okay, Blythe, are you ready to go for a swim?"

Now the only sound I could hear was the murmur of the pool's filter. Suddenly, I realized what might have happened. My heart skipped a beat.

"Blythe! Blythe!" I called urgently.

She didn't reply.

For the first time in my life, I saw myself as most other people see a blind person—helpless in a situation like this.

I grabbed at the hope that Blythe had run back to the house to get a towel or something. But what was that splash I'd heard? No, I thought, she must have fallen in.

I was seized by panic. My little daughter was drowning. I jumped into the pool and started to thrash the water as I cried her name. "Blythe! Blythe! Where are you? Answer me!"

"Oh, God," I prayed, "please help me find her. Please help me."

Suddenly, I had a thought—the kind of thought that comes to us like a bolt from the blue at a moment like this. I suddenly remembered the day at Cape Cod when Patty and I went swimming and she had called out, "See if you can catch me." I remembered how I had put my head under the water and listened for the bubbles that come with exhaling air.

I did the same thing now. I kept quite still. The surface of the pool calmed. Then I put my head under the water and listened.

Sure enough, I heard the sound of bubbles—very faintly. The sound was coming from the deep end of the pool. I swam toward the sound. Then I stopped swimming and listened again.

"Blip! Blip! Blip!"

The sound from the bubbles was louder now. Then my foot kicked out and touched something at the bottom of the pool. It was Blythe. I lifted her to the surface and swam with her to the side of the pool. I called her name again.

"Blythe! Blythe! Answer me!" I pleaded.

But she didn't. The only sound was that of water dripping from her cold limp body to the pavement below.

When I was eleven years old I had learned lifesaving

at school. I had never dreamed that I would ever have to use the lessons. Memory of the lifesaving lessons flashed back from the past. Instinctively I acted. I placed Blythe's body on the hot tiles and I pressed gently on her chest to expel water from her lungs. Then I placed my mouth over hers and breathed into her. I could feel my breath filling her lungs. Just as I had been taught many years before, I continued to breathe slowly and rhythmically into Blythe's mouth.

Blythe's life hung by a thread and I had to keep that thread from breaking.

I don't know how long it was, perhaps three minutes, before I felt Blythe's body give a little tremble. She made a very soft sound, a sort of "coooh."

It was the loveliest sound I have ever heard in my life, lovelier than any music. It was the sound of a human being reaching out for life.

A moment or two later, Blythe began to breathe on her own. I had saved her life!

Epilogue

You often hear people say that school days are the best days of your life. That's not true—at least it's not for me. I have found every year more exciting than the last. Perhaps this is because I have followed my dream—of being a composer and singer. You may have seen me on television or in a movie. Perhaps you have one of my records.

I am sure that if anyone really wants to reach a goal, he or she will get there in the end. Disappointments only mean that you've got to try harder. I guess I'm very obstinate. When people tell me that I can't do something because I'm blind, that makes me more determined than ever. For instance, some people said that I could never play golf because I'd never seen a golf ball. But I borrowed some golf clubs and practiced swinging until my arms ached and until I had blisters on my fingers. Recently I competed in a national golf tournament. I didn't win, but I had a great time.

It's hard to say what have been the most exciting moments of my life, because there have been so many of them. What a thrill it was to win the top prize at the

National Music Festival in Tokyo, Japan. It is the biggest music festival in the world, and I sang my own song. The huge crowd in the auditorium gave me a ten-minute standing ovation.

I've sung to bigger audiences than that. I was invited to sing the National Anthem at the 1976 Super Bowl in Miami. There were eighty thousand people in the stadium and another eighty million watching me on TV.

I've been in films, too. In the movie *Airport 1977* I play the part of a blind pianist. A Hollywood studio is now making a movie of my own life. In this film you will see many of the stories I have told in my book.

I don't know what is going to happen to me next year or the year after that. One day I would like to get into politics because I feel there are so many things that are wrong and that can be put right. We've got to clean the air, the rivers, and the seas. We've got to find work for everyone who wants to work—including people like me who are handicapped. I don't think we should be content until we know, for example, that no child anywhere in the world ever goes to bed hungry at night.

So you see, there is so much to do, so much to reach for. The people who make me angry are those who say we cannot find solutions to the problems of the world. Of course we can. It is the new generation that will find many of the answers. That's why I say that the most exciting and challenging years are ahead.

I hope the story of a blind boy who was told he couldn't do things other kids could do but who went

Epilogue

ahead and did them anyway will help many people to have confidence in themselves and to share my own excitement about the future.

Every morning when I wake up I cannot wait to find out what new adventures the day will hold for me. It may be talking to a group of students (and I talk to thousands of them), or it may be performing at a concert, or it may be making a film, or skydiving, or galloping a horse, or even writing a book like this!

But the moments I look forward to most—my happiest moments—are the moments I spend with my family. I love to be with Patty, perhaps walking with her along the beach below my home and listening to the surf and sea gulls. I love teaching Blythe how to play the piano or helping her with her gymnastics. She is becoming a very good gymnast. I love wrestling with Tom Sullivan III. He is my little son, two years younger than Blythe. I look forward to taking him to the spook house and taking him sailing and showing him how to catch a fish.

Little Tommy's eyes are fresh windows on my world. He tells me about many things I cannot see. I tell him how to use his senses of touch, smell, taste, and hearing. So my little son is also discovering a world that is so much more fascinating than the world that is only seen.

Last evening after supper, Patty, Blythe, Tommy, and I were sitting in our living room. The smell of dinner was floating in from the kitchen. Heidi, my seeing-eye dog, came in and nuzzled my arm. One of my songs was being played on the radio. Patty suddenly asked, "What are you thinking, Tom?"

I paused for a long moment before I answered. Then I said, "I'm thinking I'm the luckiest guy in the world."